I'm pleased, proud, a… family for years. Ron a… …azing missionaries touching ma… …s in the far northwest wilderness, in Alaska. Ron's newest book, *Navigate Your Faith*, is a monumental resource to help the Christian family to "navigate" through the world as we know it today. It challenges the reader to navigate through news and social media, as well as various other issues, and grow genuine devotion to God. It is a book that will become a guidebook in your library for the time that we live in.

—Jim Bakker
President, PTL Television Network
www.ptlnetwork.com

This book will capture your attention, captivate your mind, and convict your spirit. Every chapter is informative and impactful, causing you to make a personal assessment on the condition of your heart and purity of your life. It feels like reading a map or an inspiring life checklist that will leave you feeling confident in the Father's grace while encouraging and empowering you stay on course and continue to strive for a higher level of excellence and holiness.

—Beckah Shae
Shae Shoc Records
beckahshae.com

In his new book, *Navigate Your Faith*, Ron Pratt combines a compelling narrative with unerring truth from God's Word. In a day when solid dependence on truth and traditional values seems unheard of, the story line in this new book weaves in Biblical truth that will help any wanderer find appropriate questions and observations that will assuredly provide direction and guidance. Ron's history and life experiences make him a perfect storyteller who will inspire the reader to evaluate their motives and decisions. A great read for the young people of this culture.

—SCOTT ERICKSON
LEAD PASTOR
PEOPLES CHURCH, SALEM, OR

I have had the honor of knowing and working alongside Ron Pratt for over fifteen years. He is a powerful communicator, a loyal mentor, a passionate minister of the gospel, and a father to a fatherless generation. Ron addresses hot-button issues in the church with humor and creative storytelling, speaking transformational truths to a world full of compromise. In *Navigate Your Faith*, you will be captivated by the tale of Jason and Cindy as they face various challenges in their marriage, family, and beliefs. There are so many nuggets of truth to discover as you weave your way through this book! I fully believe that the powerful message contained in these pages will inspire, challenge, and motivate you to pursue a life more devoted to Christ.

—CHARIS LINCOLN
SOCIAL MEDIA INFLUENCER
CHARISMA STAR
WWW.CHARISMASTAR.COM

We are living in such confusing times. Many believers have struggled to understand and balance today's culture with matters of faith and traditional values. However, here is a refreshing message of reason and clarity that helps translate spiritual concepts into a language everyone can comprehend. Ron Pratt's book *Navigate Your Faith: A Christian's Field Guide to Not Getting Lost* tells the story of a young couple's search and discovery of truth in our world of conflicting ideals. The reader can quickly relate to their questions and struggles and how they found their answers in God's Word. This well-written, easy-reading guide enables anyone to learn how to live the Christian life, without being misled by modern trends of compromise and corruption. I've known this author for over twenty-five years, and I enthusiastically endorse the discoveries and insights he shares in all his writings.

—DR. DALE A. ROBBINS
PASTOR, AUTHOR, SPEAKER
PRESIDENT/FOUNDER OF THE INTERNATIONAL PRAYER NETWORK

I have known Ron for many years. His heart for the lost and his unique ways of ministering to the wonderful people of Alaska are an example to all who know him. *Navigate Your Faith: A Christian's Field Guide to Not Getting Lost* will encourage and give you insights about the exciting life of living by faith. The stories that Ron so aptly tells bring the reader deep insights about God's loving hand on their life.

—DR. WAYDE GOODALL
EXECUTIVE DIRECTOR, COMPASSION CONSORTIUM,
CONVOY OF HOPE
STRATEGIC PASTORAL ADVISOR, FOCUS ON THE FAMILY

NAVIGATE YOUR FAITH

A Christian's Field Guide
to Not Getting Lost

RON PRATT

@PapaBearAlaska

CHARISMA
HOUSE

NAVIGATE YOUR FAITH by Ron Pratt
Published by Charisma House
Charisma Media/Charisma House Book Group
600 Rinehart Road
Lake Mary, Florida 32746
www.charismahouse.com

Unless otherwise noted, all Scripture quotations are taken from the New American Standard Bible, copyright © 1960, 1962, 1963, 1968, 1971, 1972, 1973, 1975, 1977, 1995 by The Lockman Foundation. Used by permission. (www.Lockman.org)

Scripture quotations marked AMPC are from the Amplified Bible, Classic Edition. Copyright © 1954, 1958, 1962, 1964, 1965, 1987 by The Lockman Foundation. Used by permission.

Scripture quotations marked KJV are from the King James Version of the Bible.

Scripture quotations marked MSG are from The Message: The Bible in Contemporary English, copyright © 1993, 1994, 1995, 1996, 2000, 2001, 2002. Used by permission of NavPress Publishing Group.

Scripture quotations marked NIV are taken from the Holy Bible, New International Version®, NIV®. Copyright © 1973, 1978,

Visit the author's website at www.RonPrattAlaska.com or www .tgmALASKA.com.

Library of Congress Cataloging-in-Publication Data

Names: Pratt, Ron, 1961- author.
Title: Navigate your faith / by Ron Pratt.
Description: Lake Mary, Florida : Charisma House, [2019] | Includes
   bibliographical references.
Identifiers: LCCN 2018052944 (print) | LCCN 2019000039 (ebook) | ISBN
   9781629995724 (e-book) | ISBN 9781629995717 (trade paper) | ISBN
   9781629995724 (ebk.)
Subjects: LCSH: Christian life. | Christianity and culture. | Spiritual
   life--Christianity.
Classification: LCC BV4501.3 (ebook) | LCC BV4501.3 .P7325 2019 (print) | DDC
   248.4--dc23
LC record available at https://lccn.loc.gov/2018052944

19 20 21 22 23 — 987654321
Printed in the United States of America

Often a book will be dedicated to the one who most inspired the writing or to dear friends or relatives who align themselves with the concepts of the story. In the case of *Navigate Your Faith* my inspiration came from many unsuspecting people from my past and present.

Although the idea and content came as a direct download from the Holy Spirit in the middle of the night, I recognize that such downloads from heaven come from consistent investments of prayer.

Many have invested in prayer over me through the years, but there is one person who stands out in a lifelong prayer commitment. My heart is filled with great love and appreciation for this special woman of God. It is my profound honor to dedicate this book to my mother, Betty Jean Pratt.

My parents regularly committed to lift me up in prayer, whether I thought I needed it or not. I will forever cherish their combined support.

CONTENTS

INTRODUCTION

THEY WANTED THE blessings of God in their lives without any personal sacrifice. *We live under grace and how we live is up to us* was their heart view. They believed their job was to enjoy the lifestyle they desired. Jesus' job was simply to stamp His approval on every expression of that lifestyle. The cultural posture that protected this perspective came easily until the careful weave of their world began to fray.

The foundational beliefs of the Western church have undergone major changes over the past few decades, with those changes accelerating in recent years. Where the American church once influenced our culture, it has now relinquished its influence *to* the culture. Heroes of the faith have been replaced by the heroes of entertainment. We have forgotten the words of our church fathers and placed commensurate value in the words of professional athletes and Hollywood actors.

Although marriages within the church are stronger than those outside of it, the enemy targets the family unit in alarming and relentless ways. Christian families have gradually abandoned biblical values and all too often have fully embraced worldly beliefs and a high tolerance of sin. The Western church aids and appeases these altered values and helps in selling Jesus as an add-on to a preferred way of living within the culture.

Father God desires true freedom, real healing, and heavenly blessing for each person and family on this earth. Just maybe that freedom should start with us, the Christian family, which consists of people like you and me who live one day and one decision at a time.

Come and journey now with Jason and Cindy Smith as they navigate life's alluring pressures and find their way to the very real and loving Creator.

CHAPTER 1
THE CHRISTIAN FAMILY

If you have been raised up with Christ, keep seeking the things above, where Christ is, seated at the right hand of God. Set your mind on the things above, not on the things that are on earth.

—COLOSSIANS 3:1–2

THEY WENT TO church most Sundays but largely out of obligation. This Sunday was not much different from the rest. They dragged themselves out of bed, told each other they wouldn't be late again—but who were they kidding?

Their Saturday ritual was no help. After a trip to the mall they attended the last showing at the cinema, so a late Saturday night was to be expected. If they did make it to Sunday morning service, the afternoon football party at the Johnsons' would be on their minds. The Johnsons always threw a great party for their "inner circle" from the church. Oh, they were open to newbies joining the group as long as they were open-minded and not all bogged down by religion.

You see, the Johnsons and their friends were "free" and living the good life.

Today was a particularly important Sunday for Jason and

1

Cindy: their NFL team was contending for a playoff spot. They conspired ahead of time to slip out of the service early in case their pastor got a little too anointed and went long. "We aren't going to be late for this game day," Cindy thought as the pastor preached through his notes.

She and Jason had invested much planning and anticipation in the game. Their new football jerseys alone cost more than they ever expected! But the investment was well worth it. After all, football was their "thing," and they were convinced their priorities made perfect sense.

"Let's stay on schedule, babe," Cindy whispered to Jason as she pointed to her Rolex. "We can slip out when they pray."

"The Johnsons snuck out a few minutes ago," Jason whispered back.

"Trained Up"

Jason Smith met Cindy Walters in college shortly after he moved from the Bible Belt to the West Coast. He grew up in a very strict religious home but never really understood the King James Version of the Bible, the only translation he was allowed to open. He had struggled in high school English class and never caught on to the archaic dialect of the King James.

Jason was turned off by a religious system that forced him to carry a Bible he didn't understand. He was equally turned off by a church that failed to understand him. He had heard far too many sermons preaching against other Bible versions and other Christian beliefs. As far as Jason was concerned, church was dead and pastors spent more time publicly criticizing other ministries than helping those around them.

Jason's move to the West Coast and his breaking away from all that controlling religiosity felt liberating! This "fresh" Christian perspective seemed so opposite to his upbringing.

He recalled the weirdness he felt when Grandma Taylor looked over her reading glasses with a disappointed glare if he dared to speak out of turn in Sunday school class. She was so different at home, always cooking and seeming to enjoy having kids around. In the classroom, however, she transformed into a frustrated old woman who apparently felt called to portray the anger of God, especially toward little boys. Jason's gang of young peers secretly referred to her as "The Transformer." While the home-made cookies she brought to the monthly church potlucks were absolutely heavenly, the boys were convinced the ruler she wielded in Sunday school had been made by the devil himself!

Unlike Jason, Cindy was born and raised in Southern California. As was common in many families, her mother was the only spiritual figure in the home and was 100 percent devoted to the "religion" of shopping! If the mall was a church, Cindy's mother would be considered a faithful pillar, investing her time, passion, and resources with great devotion.

Cindy's father was virtually nonexistent in her life. He would not be burdened with religious obligations or tedious family functions but kept his focus where it should be—on money, making money, and making *more* money. His invest-ment firm had done quite well, often keeping him away from home and for the most part distant from his daughter's life.

When she lived at home, Cindy went to church with her mom as faithfully as their social and shopping life would permit. She had a Bible and enjoyed reading it on occasion, especially *The Message*, which was much easier to grasp than her old Bible from childhood. Cindy was fairly familiar with its pages but was much better versed in the sport of online shop-ping. The credit card her father provided to compensate for his absence made shopping easy. At a young age she learned the power of that magical piece of plastic. She believed it was her responsibility to shop. Paying off the bill was not her concern; that was Daddy's problem!

The Bible says that if you "train up a child in the way he should go, even when he is old he will not depart from it" (Prov. 22:6). I have often wondered whether a child is influenced only when trained up in the way he or she *should* go or also when trained in the way he or she *should not* go. Cindy was definitely "trained up" but more effectively by Hollywood than by the church. Her favorite movie stars had more influence on her desires, directions, and dreams than Jesus did.

After her parents dragged her through their painful divorce, Cindy felt numb to life and had little reason to trust others. Like every young girl she wanted to be loved and protected by her dad. Now that he was out of the house, she had more freedom than ever before. He had never given her any real restrictions or guidelines, and he never screened her boyfriends. On the outside she might have resisted such constraints from her father, but in her heart she wanted someone—especially her daddy—to care enough to create a safe zone.

Deep within the heart of a young girl is the desire for Daddy's protection. When this foundational need is unmet, others tend to fill that position. Most of these people go by the title *boyfriend*, but whatever their titles, they are underqualified and ill-equipped for the task. In the absence of a dad's impartation in the spiritual role of "training up" the child, the child's heart becomes open to training from others. In the crucial adolescent years the child becomes a sponge, quick to absorb love in any available form.

Trained up—Cindy surely was! She was trained with excellence by a world focused on entertainment. She had learned to make decisions from the perspective that asks, "Will it be fun for me? Will it be entertaining? Did Sunday's sermon suit my taste?"

The "spirit of entertainment" (as I like to call it) promotes self-focus and personal indulgence. This faulty training develops a mind-set that measures all activities and relationships by the standard of self-gratification. To Cindy, Jesus didn't seem to offer much of that. While she tried to make a little room for Him in her life, the concept of His lordship was far too radical and was reserved for "overzealous" Christians.

In much the way early Christians were trained up by the Torah (the first five books of the Bible), many like Cindy have been trained up by media. Early Christians talked about Scripture and prophecy; modern Christians are more prone to discussing their favorite movies, even reciting lines from them word for word. **If the movie theater were a church, then its success in growing a congregation would be second to none.**

Jason and Cindy each brought their life training into their marriage. Shortly after their wedding Jason agreed to go to church with Cindy. The church was growing rapidly and was made up of mostly younger families close to their age. What a refreshing change it was from his past church experience! This "seeker-friendly" setting was casual and inviting. The social opportunities were endless, and no one ever got in your face with religious pressure.

Nothing is worse than mixing church with your personal life was this couple's view. That belief worked for Jason, who wasn't really concerned with the confusing details of spiritual

5

growth. Because of his strict religious upbringing he believed he was "good to go." In other words his eternal future was secure no matter how he lived. "What's the point?" he often wondered. If his confession at Bible camp many years earlier was all it took, then he was sure no lifestyle adjustments were necessary. Nothing needed to change.

Predictably Cindy connected with several like-minded shopping enthusiasts from the church, which kept any potential boredom from creeping into her life. The shopping was not limited to the mall. Cindy also "shopped" the church services she attended and gave each of them a rating. It was like a sport to her! The first and most important factor in rating the service involved who was in attendance. Nearly as important was what they were wearing and how the interaction went.

For Jason it was all about how well the band performed. He had dabbled in music as a teen and occasionally strummed a few chords on the guitar. On Sunday, music was what captivated his attention. If the sounds were good, Jason was satisfied.

———————•———————

I would propose that what I call the spirit of entertainment might be a more widespread addiction than any other substance abuse or bad habit in the church. Although Christians don't wear "Entertain Me!" T-shirts to Sunday service, the *spirit* of this desire is alive and well.

One element of the entertainment mind-set is revealed in the tendency to criticize. The art of critique has its place, especially when it is invited. The critique of an editor, for example, is essential in helping authors to clearly deliver their messages (so true in the case of this book!). However, unsolicited critique can be out of place and is often fueled by a spirit of criticism.

I've heard it said that "the habit of criticism grows as faith declines."[1] According to the dictionary, to be *critical* is to be "inclined to find fault or to judge with severity, often too readily; occupied with or skilled in criticism."[2]

Just to clarify, criticalness is *not* one of the spiritual gifts. Furthermore, where criticism is found, generosity is often lacking. I truly believe faith and giving are linked. Christians with a strong faith in God's Word are also strong believers in the heart of giving who demonstrate generosity through their lifestyle.

Stay with me. I'm heading somewhere.

Give or Take?

When the early New Testament church gathered, it was more like a potluck and less like a restaurant. Everyone at a potluck brings something to the table. The focus is not on what you can get but what you can *give*. The Christian mind-set today often resembles the restaurant model—no preparation is needed! Just come through the door, bring nothing but your-self, find a good seat, place your order, and rate the meal (and if warranted, complain about the service). This selfish appe-tite for personal entertainment has infiltrated the church at every level.

In counseling a young lady who was completely submersed in the world of entertainment, my wife and I challenged her to a thirty-day "media fast"—no television, no movies, no downloads, and no social media. She resisted strongly and refused to consider such a challenge. Even after we reduced the abstinence to a single week, she looked at us with tears in her eyes and said, "I can't do that."

What an eye-opener it was!

This spirit of entertainment is fueled by fierce and unhealthy selfishness. A self-centered heart always makes life decisions by asking, "What will be the most fun for *me*?"

One Sunday after service at a church where I served on staff, I approached a longtime church leader to solicit his help with an evangelistic youth event. I explained that the outreach would require a few adults assisting in a variety of areas. Without any hesitation he answered, "I'll pray about it."

Being well-versed in "Christianese," I understood what he was really saying: "I'm not interested, but I want to appear spiritual. So to buy myself some time and to (hopefully) give you a chance to forget that you ever asked me, I will tell you that I'm making this a matter of prayer."

Amazingly, as he turned around to leave, another man in the church approached him and asked, "Would you like to join our church softball team? We meet twice a week in the evenings for practice and every Saturday for games all summer."

The man quickly answered, "Sure! Sounds great."

It was obvious the youth outreach pegged lower on his "fun meter" than softball did. It is funny how a season of "prayer" is needed to obey the command of God, but for entertainment's sake we pull instantaneous decisions out of thin air and see no need to run them through any God-approved filters.

I can recall many conversations over the years along these lines:

"Will you be signing up for our summer mission trip?"

"Maybe, unless something else comes up."

The *something else* was not referring to a work-related assignment but an entertaining activity of some sort. The issue was which activity would score highest on the person's fun meter. That is the thought process for those influenced by the spirit of entertainment. The biblical thought process is quite the opposite and leads to this warning: "Do not love the world nor the things in the world. If anyone loves the world, the love of the Father is not in him" (1 John 2:15).

———————◆———————

Jason and Cindy wished their pastor would make life easy for them and close the service "on time." Then they could catch their breath and stop at the house to change into those new jerseys before each game. As it turned out, the pastor did not preach long on this particular Sunday. During the short drive to the Johnsons' house, Jason surmised, "Maybe Pastor ended on time because his team is playing this afternoon."

Everything was what Jason and Cindy hoped for that Sunday: The football party could not have been better. They spent the day with great friends and plenty of delicious food, and to top it off, their team was still in the running and would be playing the next Sunday!

The Smiths eagerly agreed to host the following week's party at their house. They could do it as well as anyone, but there was no time to waste and much planning to do. Of course some shopping would be in order, so within three minutes of walking in the door, Cindy started a list of party supplies and mapped out the game room. Meanwhile Jason attacked the next level of his new race-car video game.

Little did they know that the next game day would have a major impact on their lives.

CHAPTER 2
THE MEDIA TRAP

Moreover, man does not know his time: like fish
caught in a treacherous net and birds trapped in
a snare, so the sons of men are ensnared at an
evil time when it suddenly falls on them.
—ECCLESIASTES 9:12

"**G**ETTING READY FOR the big game, I see," Cindy said with a touch of sarcasm.

It was Thursday night, and Jason's eyes were glued to the screen. The sports channel was his favorite prep source for the game. The bikini challenge segment was nothing but a harmless interlude Jason would patiently endure for the sake of his preparation.

"Hey, it's just part of the show, baby. It'll be over in a few."

Cindy rolled her eyes and continued transforming the den into the ultimate party venue. Nothing would get in the way of this event, and nobody would outdo Cindy.

Struggling to remove a large painting, she looked over at Jason, his eyes still glued to the bikini challenge. "This is serious business, Jason!" she hollered. "Come help me with this."

Entering a Net

Recently I viewed an inspirational video on YouTube. It was very moving to watch a friend of mine share the message of Jesus with the thousands who packed out a stadium. As the video ended, a list of "related videos" appeared on the right-hand side of the screen.

Simply click and view some additional great ministry, right?

Not exactly. The list of so-called "related videos" started with two more videos of my friend ministering. The third selection, however, involved a young woman who was struggling to keep her surgically enhanced body packed into her undersized bikini. I am sure this video had nothing to do with international ministry, yet according to YouTube it was "related."

Every day we are surrounded with opportunities to compromise our integrity. Television is an obvious culprit. So is the internet, which is a "one click and there it is" temptation. To be clear, I am not advocating against technologies such as YouTube. In fact all of our ministry videos are posted on this convenient online platform. The problem is that without a personal standard—an obvious line drawn in the sand—anything goes and the enemy can easily access us.

In essence an entire generation of Christians is being raised by YouTube and other internet influences. The word *internet* breaks easily into two parts: *inter* and *net*. That should be a clue! Humans have made nets for thousands of years, and new technology means today's nets can be used with extreme accuracy. You can even buy a net gun, a device that launches a net thirty yards or so to restrain an animal as large as an elk.

Historically nets have been used mostly to catch fish, but some nets were made by indigenous people in North America to catch animals—even large animals! I recall listening to an Athabascan Indian elder tell stories about how his people made large nets from green root systems and positioned them strategically to snag caribou in mountain draws.

Yes, *caribou!* The Native people would locate natural bottlenecks where animals migrated down mountains or canyons. To catch them, the hunters would attach their nets to trees high off the ground. The caribou were accustomed to using their large antlers to move small trees, brush, and other debris out of their way. The nets would entangle their antlers, trapping the animals long enough for the hunters to finish the job and harvest the meat for their people.

Obviously the *net* does not work until the animal *enters* it. *Inter-net* really is a clue!

———————◆———————

Jason's movie collection looked like a video rental store. Name the title and he probably had it. There were no X-rated films in his collection, but with no kids in the house pretty much anything else was acceptable. Their friends were impressed with Jason's amazing selection, so the Smiths' home became the favored location for movie night, a social event that was happening more and more often.

Jason and Cindy viewed their favorite films many times over, to the point that they could recite complete lines from any of them. Although Cindy was more open-minded than most, even teasing other ladies at church for being prudish, she did not always feel comfortable with Jason's movie choices. Watching sexually explicit scenes might be the norm in the twenty-first century, but they challenged Cindy's inner boundaries. When things got more graphic than she liked, she often snuck into the kitchen to make freshly buttered popcorn, just the way Jason liked it.

"If the sex bothers you, don't watch it!" Jason would holler as Cindy left the room.

Jason was truly hooked on cinema. When he wasn't projecting a favorite film on their stunning home theater equipment, Jason would view movies and videos on his new laptop. Many scenes were embedded in his mind, and he could recount one after another with total accuracy. These scenes and his many memorized movie quotes were good filler for almost any conversation.

———————◆———————

While women are relationally driven, men are (by design) visually driven. Men don't always remember what they hear (just ask my wife!). And they don't always remember what they read or smell. But men remember what they see. Being driven by what they see is in the male DNA. Without much effort they can recall what they have witnessed in the past. Remember: King David's big mistake happened after he saw Bathsheba's private moments with his natural eyes.

I remember working in construction with a friend in the late 1970s. We were thrilled to have a five-dollar-an-hour summer job cleaning up after construction crews that had stormed through the floor of a high-rise building. One day while cleaning out piles of construction debris, we came across a magazine left behind by a worker. As I scooped it up with my large shovel and tossed it into the wheelbarrow, it opened to a centerfold picture that "scared the tar" out of these two church boys! We argued about who would throw away the magazine and then buried it under rubble in the dumpster.

Yet that centerfold image stuck in my memory banks for years to come.

Media has come a long way since the 1970s. The fear that someone will catch you taking a dirty magazine out of your mailbox is no more. Today you can get images with the click of a button in the privacy of your own home.

So let's talk about the World Wide Web.

"Oh no," you say, "there he goes again!"

Not really, so stay with me. I truly appreciate the web. It is wonderful for research and an amazing way to promote ministry. Thanks to the web we can share the life-altering story of Jesus with people all around the world, in hundreds of languages, 24/7—for little to no cost! The web has become a powerful tool in the hands of God's people.

As long as technology continues to advance, the thief will try to use it against God's people.

Yet it is also a powerful tool used by the devil, who has a threefold plan to steal, kill, and destroy people everywhere. Jesus said it in John 10:10, "The thief comes only to steal and kill and destroy; I came that they may have life, and have it abundantly." As long as technology continues to advance, the thief will try to use it against God's people.

I am sure you know this, but please bear with me. Webs are made by spiders, who weave them for one purpose: to capture prey. Spiders create webs in high-traffic areas *to entangle* insects. Once a spider snags its victim, it injects a venom to paralyze and liquefy it from the inside out. That might be overly graphic, but it is real. As predators go, spiders are fierce. A quick Google search yields ample footage of deadly spiders sucking the life out of their helpless captives. (I was surprised to learn, in fact, that some large spiders can even capture birds in their very strong webs.)

The bottom line? Webs are designed by predators to do five things: entangle, capture, infect, kill, and consume their prey! The enemy of our souls effectively uses the World Wide Web to do just that. His intentions for an unassuming and often unaware generation of Christians are very strategic, so let me break down the five steps in his "media trap."

Entangle

Entanglement is not the enemy's end goal; it is the first step of the process. Nets accomplish the task of ensnaring the spider's prey well. In most cases the victim becomes more entangled the harder it attempts to get free. Without outside help it is unlikely to regain its freedom, and movement in the web serves only to alert the spider to its success.

One of the enemy's best snares for humans is an independent spirit, which convinces us to try and fix things on our own. Pride tends to keep us from seeking help from others or even admitting we need it. Yet *we were designed* to need other people's help. It has been that way from the beginning. When God created Adam, He knew the man needed a helper—and so do we.

I once found a butterfly entangled in a spider web and struggling to get free, so I used a twig to help it along. The delicate creature was just barely stuck, but absent outside help it was stuck enough to remain hostage. Freeing the butterfly took very little physical effort on my part. My outside perspective helped the cause and gave me (and the butterfly) the advantage.

Surprisingly, when Christians seek help from others, they often look to those who are entangled in the very same (or at least a very similar) web. They essentially rely on the "blind leading the blind," when what they really need is an outside-the-web perspective from someone who is not ensnared with what holds them captive.

Like the spider the enemy spins very attractive webs, and too many Christians are lured by them. We can learn something about the enemy's tricks from examples in nature. Take, for example, orb-weaving spiders. They use visual attractions such as bright, ultraviolet-light-reflecting silk to encourage one-way flights into their lairs. The webbing looks inviting and safe from a distance, and curiosity lures the victim close enough to get caught.

For the Smith family and millions of other families similar attractions are woven into the culture of entertainment. I can remember an early bra commercial on TV in which a woman wore the undergarment on the outside of her clothing. At the time even that was considered improper for a young boy to see. Television has come a long way, baby, and the *way* was forged by desensitizing successive generations to what is appropriate and what is not. We have gone from seemingly innocent advertising to provocative lingerie ads that get right up in your face!

Some might say, "That doesn't bother me. I'm a strong Christian. I can handle it!"

Is it possible that being strong enough to handle worldly influences *in* your life is not as important as being strong and wise enough to screen worldliness *out* of your life?

Infect

Physical infections typically start from something very small—a bite, a puncture, or a microscopic organism often is to blame. I recently read an interesting article, "10 Infectious

Diseases That Changed History." All of them began from a microscopic virus, bacteria, or parasite:[1]

1. Cholera

2. Ebola

3. Malaria

4. Tuberculosis

5. HIV/AIDS

6. Syphilis

7. Polio

8. Spanish influenza

9. Smallpox

10. Bubonic plague

Now think about the spider: once the prey is trapped in its web, the spider "infects" it with a poison that attacks the nervous system and causes paralysis. The "infection" results directly from the predator's injection. The victim is still alive but helpless; it remains aware, but it is powerless to act.

Many "infections" are transmitted in today's entertainment culture. According to the RAND Corporation, "the average American teenager watches three hours of television every day. Typical teen fare contains heavy doses of sexual content, ranging from touching, kissing, jokes, and innuendo to conversations about sexual activity and portrayals of intercourse. Sex is often presented as a casual activity without risk or consequences."[2]

Yet while television may have been the babysitter of a former generation, the format of media consumption is morphing.

The graph below shows a steady decline in TV viewership as internet usage climbs.[3]

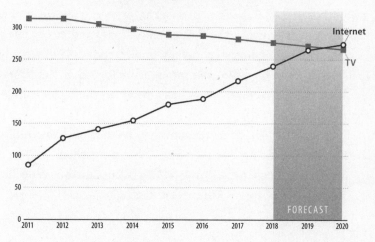

Minutes of Daily TV and Internet Consumption in US

The spiritual infection is the same, whether it is "injected" by a TV set, computer, or mobile device. Like a physical infection it starts small and goes undetected for a time. If it goes untreated, however, it can lead to death. The spiritual infection hidden in our entertainment culture is the secularization that is slowly poisoning the church with compromise, self-focus, fear of man, disregard for life, sin tolerance, lust of the flesh, jealousy, and rebellion. I propose to you that this spiritual infection is killing a generation faster than the diseases on the previous list. And if not treated, this growing infection can change history for the worse.

Capture

After it administers its numbing injection, the spider secures its prey by wrapping it in layers of fresh webbing. If there had been even the slightest chance of the victim breaking free from its entanglement, this feature ensures its demise.

Although television has gradually but powerfully eroded our morals over the decades, the potential influence of internet programming is virtually limitless. With laptops, smartphones, and other personal devices, people can privately see what they want when they want it without being discovered or censored. Again, I am not against technology or electronics—I'm writing this book on an iPad! But the same technology that has simplified our lives in so many ways has also given the "spider" huge opportunities.

Even in the Christian community, media is a controlling influence, capturing families and "wrapping them up" in a counterfeit subculture within the Christian culture. Whether we admit it or not, it is killing families.

Kill

The spider's victim dies a slow, inevitable death. It is to the spider's advantage to keep the body and blood fresh during liquefaction.

The media trap does not kill Christians overnight; it is a slow, gradual undermining that usually goes undetected until the damage is done. You could compare it to the collapse of a bridge or roadway, which seems to happen in a moment, quick and without warning. When the structure gives way, the effects of the undermining are obvious, but a process preceded the disaster. Foundational erosion had to occur over seasons or years. Without regular maintenance, inspections, and testing, the hidden damage continues to worsen until it is tragically exposed, too late to spare its victims.

Consume

This is the spider's ultimate purpose: consume as much of the victim as possible. Depending on the arachnid's species and size, the captured meal will last mere minutes or many days. Even after the prey is consumed, the remains of the prey in the web can attract other potential prey to the scene.

We have an enemy that works in even more personal ways. He hates us, and his hatred fuels his predatory, five-step plan. His consumption of families serves a greater purpose, and he wants the spectacle of the "meal" to last as long as possible. He knows the longer he feeds on his prey, the more people he can influence, because every human being has relational influence.

One person's choices impact many other people. One person's physical or spiritual death serves as a template for the demise of others. We were created to be relational. Therefore, our connections can lure other people into what we perceive to be safe and attractive webs. Our losses, whether physical or spiritual, fuel the untruths the father of lies speaks to the people we know and love.

In other words our failures give others permission to fail, just as our successes exemplify success for them. Whether we make good or bad choices, someone will follow in our footsteps. Even when we are unaware of it, someone is following us; it may be from a distance, but we are indeed being followed.

> Therefore, since we have so great a cloud of witnesses surrounding us, let us also lay aside every encumbrance and the sin which so easily *entangles* us, and let us run with endurance the race that is set before us, fixing our eyes on Jesus, the author and perfecter of faith, who for the joy set before Him endured the cross, despising the shame, and has sat down at the right hand of the throne of God.
> —HEBREWS 12:1–2, EMPHASIS ADDED

Fixing our attention on Jesus and allowing Him to perfect our faith are the best defenses against demonic entrapment. Our ability to resist deception is strengthened when we ask the Holy Spirit to develop our God-given discernment, both to expose the enemy's inner workings and to help us perceive the greatness of our holy God with renewed clarity.

CHAPTER 3
A NEWFOUND FREEDOM

Stand fast therefore in the liberty by which Christ has made us free, and do not be entangled again with a yoke of bondage.
—GALATIANS 5:1, NKJV

PREPARATIONS FOR THE football party progressed nicely. Some extra decorations and a new team mural topped off the ambience. The party at the Smiths' home was shaping up to be epic.

The big day came quickly and church with it. Jason and Cindy prayed it wouldn't happen, but the service ran long anyway. As they had planned to do ahead of time, they slipped out early.

"We can't be late today. We're the party hosts!" Jason exclaimed under his breath.

Back at the house friends started arriving. As the food parade from the kitchen picked up steam, Jason packed ice over what appeared to be a truckload of soda. This was going to be another great day with friends—especially if their team played well!

The Johnsons showed up a tad late, decked out in football fashion. (Apparently the Smiths' jersey craze had caught on!) Surprisingly, they brought a new couple along, but they were very upbeat and seemed just as excited about the game as everybody else. Cindy knew there would be enough food to feed a small army, so unexpected guests would be just fine. The new couple didn't come empty-handed either—they brought a cooler with enough beer to go around the room several times.

Jason had never been a drinker, having made it through college with minimal exposure to alcohol. He could credit his abstinence to three factors: One, his after-school job kept him socially disconnected. Two, his roommate was one of those "radical Holy Spirit guys" who personally guaranteed that no alcohol would ever enter their room. And three, he was afraid Grandma Taylor would leap through the dorm window, ruler in hand, and stare him down with her ninja eyes of fire!

Cindy, on the other hand, started drinking in high school but made a decision to stop when the special speaker at a college retreat shared some eye-opening stories. Cindy truly sensed God's touch that day and made a commitment to the Lord to keep alcohol out of her life. To her glad surprise the desire to drink completely left her shortly after that encounter.

Now years later things were changing for the Smiths. After a short sermon from their new young guests on the biblical view of drinking from Ephesians 5:18—"Do not get drunk with wine"—they all agreed that the sin is not in the social consumption of alcohol but in getting drunk. Anything is good in moderation, right?

Intrigued by a new level of freedom, Jason had a beer and would later make sure beer was prevalent at any gatherings he hosted. He even enjoyed a couple of beers after dinner each night. Cindy, however, still remembered the pain alcohol had once caused her. She also remembered her commitment. Choosing to drink again was still not an option for her.

Sunday football parties continued as Jason and Cindy's team did better than ever in the playoffs. But there would be no Super Bowl title this year. Finally the season ended and Sunday gatherings became less predictable.

At a barbecue the Johnsons announced they were expecting their first child. Cindy wasn't sure how to respond to the news. The Johnsons were their closest friends. The two couples did everything together! They had always made it a point to invite childless couples into their circle. Not that kids were bad of course. The Smiths just wanted to keep their freedom.

Now things would be different. Cindy wondered whether what they'd shared with the Johnsons was suddenly lost. Nevertheless she congratulated her friends as they headed to their car a little earlier than usual.

Several months passed when in conversation about the Johnsons, Jason suggested having a child might not be such a bad idea. His statement did not go over as well as he had hoped.

"I'm not going to sacrifice my body for a kid!" Cindy snapped back. She worked hard at staying fit and was not about to trade her trim figure for big hips.

The conversation was over—the baby idea was *not* going to happen.

Cindy soon loosened up in another way, however, surprising Jason when she grabbed a beer and joined him in front of his new seventy-inch HDTV. After swearing off the stuff for years, she figured, "What the heck?"

They had not hung out with the Johnsons in more than four months, and Cindy still did not know what to make of it. Although they were planning to attend the Johnsons' upcoming Fourth of July barbecue, the Smiths had (very purposely) visited with their best friends less frequently. Instead they spent more time with other couples who were "free" like they were—free from religious pressure and free from kids.

Weighing the Evidence

The most common "supporting evidence" I have heard from Christians for drinking alcohol is "Jesus turned the water into wine." Another popular justification is "If Jesus were walking the earth today, He would hang out in the bars and minister to people."

If you have been around the church for any length of time, you have probably heard the same things. As common as these statements are, however, I have yet to find a Scripture reference that clearly places our Messiah in a local bar. On the contrary, Jesus went out of His way to exemplify a life of purity for us to follow.

People are always trying to put something in the hand of Jesus to justify what they don't want to let go of. As David Wilkerson wrote in his book *Sipping Saints: A Challenge to Drinking Christians*, "Our sinless High Priest ate with publicans and sinners and drank the pure juice of the vine. But never did He sit in the seat of the scornful or touch the cup when its contents were 'red and biting.'"[1]

Father God did an amazing job creating the minds of those He made in His image. We have the natural ability to justify whatever we really want to do, have, or experience. Too often we live exactly as we desire, with the title of Christian having little bearing on the choices we make to please ourselves. As Western Christians many of us barely notice others are watching. Too easily we say, "I don't need to change for them. If they don't like how I live, that's their problem."

Before your blood starts boiling, let me make something

very clear: alcohol is not a sin, and drinking alcohol does not confirm a one-way pass to hell. Now that I have made this perfectly clear, let's move on and revisit a passage from Hebrews, with an additional verse this time:

> Therefore, since we have so great a cloud of witnesses surrounding us, let us also lay aside every encumbrance and the sin which so easily entangles us, and let us run with endurance the race that is set before us, fixing our eyes on Jesus, the author and perfecter of faith, who for the joy set before Him endured the cross, despising the shame, and has sat down at the right hand of the throne of God. For consider Him who has endured such hostility by sinners against Himself, so that you will not grow weary and lose heart.
>
> —HEBREWS 12:1–3

In verse 1 the word *encumbrance* is used in the New American Standard Bible, and the word *weight* is used in the New King James Version. The verse simply says to lay aside every weighty encumbrance and sin that can so easily entangle us. We are not the best judge of what easily entangles us. Often when we are in the trap, we cannot see it for what it is. That is how a web of deception works. We need help to recognize it, so the Holy Spirit often sends others to shed light on any dark areas in our lives. They help awaken us to places in which our eyes have slowly adjusted to darkness.

People are always trying to put something in the hand of Jesus to justify what they don't want to let go of.

An *encumbrance* is "something that encumbers; something burdensome, useless, or superfluous; burden; hindrance."[2]

With that in mind let's look at the same passage from Hebrews, in the Amplified Bible, Classic Edition this time:

> Therefore then, since we are surrounded by so great a cloud of witnesses [who have borne testimony to the Truth], let us strip off and throw aside every encumbrance (unnecessary weight) and that sin which so readily (deftly and cleverly) clings to and entangles us, and let us run with patient endurance and steady and active persistence the appointed course of the race that is set before us, looking away [from all that will distract] to Jesus, Who is the Leader and the Source of our faith [giving the first incentive for our belief] and is also its Finisher [bringing it to maturity and perfection]. He, for the joy [of obtaining the prize] that was set before Him, endured the cross, despising and ignoring the shame, and is now seated at the right hand of the throne of God. Just think of Him Who endured from sinners such grievous opposition and bitter hostility against Himself [reckon up and consider it all in comparison with your trials], so that you may not grow weary or exhausted, losing heart and relaxing and fainting in your minds.
>
> —HEBREWS 12:1–3, AMPC

The "unnecessary weight" mentioned in verse 1 slowly drags us down and keeps us from winning the race! When we slow down, a gradual buildup of debris ultimately entangles us. No one ever intends for this to happen. Most ensnared people say, "I have it under control." Over the years many have told me how they thought the situation was "no big deal." Yet before they knew it, they were in too deep, and the addiction overcame them.

Compromise influences us to systematically remove the security fences that once kept danger at a distance. It usually happens without our noticing it. As Pastor Kenny Luck wrote:

Drinking is about control. Men love to push the limit, getting as close to the cliff as possible. Unfortunately, alcohol can blur the lines, turning a black and white issue into hazy gray. It's in those gray moments we can think things, say things, and do things under the control of another "spirit." The Bible clearly states to be "sober" minded and do not get drunk so that we never surrender our body, mind or soul to anything other than God. Most of us all have stories about waking up after we've surrendered control, and it's not pretty. So we have to choose to stay away from the cliff, and be wise.[3]

In Pastor Luck's article the following scriptures help to make the matter plain:

Wine is a mocker and beer a brawler; whoever is led astray by them is not wise.

—PROVERBS 20:1, NIV

Therefore do not be foolish, but understand what the Lord's will is. Do not get drunk on wine, which leads to debauchery. Instead, be filled with the Spirit.

—EPHESIANS 5:17–18, NIV

"Pushing the limits" is part of the human condition. God designed us with an inherent desire to see how close to the edge we can get without falling off. When partnered with faith, courage is powerful. That is how men and women dare to go where no one has gone before and how people climb mountains that few would dare to summit. When the voice of God speaks, we cannot fulfill the call without this kind of faith. The tendency to go "full throttle" is coded into our DNA. God put it there to fuel the aggressive obedience needed to achieve His supernatural mandate and our life's purpose.

The problem arises when our heavenly purpose remains unknown to us. Alcohol and all addictive substances seem to bolster us for the challenges but instead leave us with the illusion of self-control. The substance doesn't necessarily push us over the cliff; it conditions us to becoming comfortable with the risks of living there.

Think about it: Would the perfect Son of God abuse His physical body with a substance that could hurt him? Of course not. He would not do anything contrary to the Father's will.

Of course the impact of alcohol is not just individual; it is global. "The harmful use of alcohol resulted in an estimated 3 million deaths...globally in 2016," which is greater than deaths from tuberculosis, HIV/AIDS, and violence combined, according to the World Health Organization (WHO).[4] The WHO also warned that alcohol consumption is increasing, annually causing one out of every twenty deaths worldwide, attributed to drunk driving as well as alcohol-related disease, violence, and other causes. According to a WHO official, this amounts to one death by alcohol every ten seconds of every day.[5]

Overall, 5.3 percent of deaths in 2016 resulted from alcohol use, whereas HIV/AIDS was responsible for less than 2 percent of all deaths that year. The WHO also notes alcohol consumption in low-income countries increases as wealth increases. Because of the negative side effects of alcohol use— including liver disease, increased susceptibility to infectious and chronic diseases, and traffic accidents (12.3 percent of all alcohol fatalities were attributable to road injuries in 2016)— people in all economic strata should find this concerning.[6]

Lead or Follow?

According to Jesus' own mandate, Christians are called to lead! Not all are chosen to lead a church or ministry, but each of us is called to lead people, especially the lost. The question is, What kind of leadership will we provide?

King Lemuel's mother taught him how to conduct himself in ways that would lead others in the right direction. The following passage reveals the king valued his mother's wisdom, as we should.

> The words of King Lemuel, the oracle which his mother taught him: What, O my son? And what, O son of my womb? And what, O son of my vows? Do not give your strength to women, or your ways to that which destroys kings. It is not for kings, O Lemuel, it is not for kings to drink wine, or for rulers to desire strong drink, for they will drink and forget what is decreed, and pervert the rights of all the afflicted. Give strong drink to him who is perishing, and wine to him whose life is bitter. Let him drink and forget his poverty and remember his trouble no more. Open your mouth for the mute, for the rights of all the unfortunate. Open your mouth, judge righteously, and defend the rights of the afflicted and needy.
>
> —PROVERBS 31:1–9

Now let's read the same passage, from *The Message*:

> The words of King Lemuel, the strong advice his mother gave him: "Oh, son of mine, what can you be thinking of! Child whom I bore! The son I dedicated to God! Don't dissipate your virility on fortune-hunting women, promiscuous women who shipwreck leaders. Leaders can't afford to make fools of themselves, gulping wine and swilling beer, lest, hung over, they don't know right from wrong, and the people who depend on them are hurt. Use wine and beer only as sedatives, to kill the pain and dull the ache of the terminally ill, for whom life is a

living death. Speak up for the people who have no voice,
for the rights of all the down-and-outers. Speak out for
justice! Stand up for the poor and destitute!"

—PROVERBS 31:1–9, MSG

As leaders in the faith we are called to be strong, sharp,
and focused in our lifestyle of helping widows, orphans, and
others in need, especially those who come seeking deliverance
from addiction.

———◆———

Even for a July Fourth weekend the grocery store was surprisingly packed. Navigating the aisles was daunting, but Cindy
was as experienced a combat shopper as anyone. Yet nothing
could have prepared her for what was next.

"Oh no! Is that the pastor's wife coming straight at me?"
Cindy wondered with alarm. She knew it was too late to duck
away. Their eyes had met and a face-to-face moment was
inevitable.

It's not that Cindy disliked Joyce. She liked and respected
her and thought being around her was a joy—which was all
the more reason for Cindy to divert Joyce's attention from the
contents of her cart. It was mission impossible, however, with
beer cartons strategically stacked on the bottom rack beneath
the basket.

Before Joyce could ask about the goodies in Cindy's basket,
Cindy quickly switched the subject to missions (Joyce's passion) and mentioned the letter she and Jason received from
a little girl they had sponsored through a program Joyce had
initiated months earlier. Until that point the Smiths had
given to missions sporadically, usually when a missionary
spoke at church. Now the sponsorship program had become

all the rage, with some families sponsoring multiple children. It was not difficult for the Smiths to participate. For the cost of a latte a day they could feed, educate, and clothe the child. And they were truly touched by the young girl's response to their commitment.

Halfway through their conversation the unthinkable happened: Joyce glanced downward, all the way to the beer stash. As she slowly raised her eyes, she said with a manufactured smile, "Looks like you're planning quite a party, Cindy."

It was as though the whole scene went *Matrix*. The echo of Joyce's statement played over and over in Cindy's head with the amplified sound of her own breathing.

A bunch of unrealistic rules was not the life of "freedom" Cindy thought Jesus died for. So she gave Joyce the default answer that had worked so effectively in the past—the one that shut down every question from overly religious people who pried into her personal life. It worked for her and Jason's movie and music choices and was now a conversation-stopper to defend their social drinking.

This time, however, Cindy felt backed into a corner (the dairy section, to be exact), and her canned answer was all she had: "We don't want to be legalistic, now do we?" she quipped with feigned confidence.

The conversation was effectively concluded. Joyce reached out for a goodbye hug, and the two women went their separate ways. Joyce did not seem judgmental or rude, and the legalism reply apparently worked like a charm.

Or did it?

As Cindy drove home, something felt different... empty. It was as though she had lost this time, but *why*? Her answer had shut up Joyce, just as it had quashed every other encounter. But for some reason Cindy could not shake off her uneasiness.

The pastor's wife's words echoed in her head: "Looks like you're planning quite a party, Cindy."

Getting the Words Right

Legalism has become a convenient catchphrase. Many professing Christians use it to defend something they want the freedom to do, see, read, attend, eat, wear, drink, or enjoy. Sadly enough this card is often played as an excuse *not* to do the right thing. It is evident in the lack of discipline administered to children and a lack of accountability within the whole body of Christ—yes, especially the adults.

The dictionary defines *legalism* as "strict adherence, or the principle of strict adherence, to law or prescription, especially to the letter rather than the spirit; [in] theology, the doctrine that salvation is gained through good works, [or] the judging of conduct in terms of adherence to precise laws; in Chinese philosophy, the principles and practices of a school of political theorists advocating strict legal control over all activities, a system of rewards and punishments uniform for all classes, and an absolute monarchy."[7]

Wow! According to that, legalism isn't very attractive—and it's not. Yet many belief systems fit this profile. In fact most religions are based on restrictive guidelines that keep their believers bound and jumping through difficult hoops in order to remain in good standing. I won't take the time to pick on these systems, but it is important to understand Christianity is not now and never was based on legalism.

When serving God is only about rules, there is a lack of relationship. God enjoyed the relational contact He had with Adam and Eve and desired relationship with everyone who came from Adam's seed. Sin disrupted the relational process and separated man from God. Ever since then Father God has desired to get us "back to the garden." He gave His Son, Jesus, for this very purpose. Evangelism is that simple: getting people back to the garden with the Father. (OK, maybe it's not a physical garden, but we will enjoy that later!)

When we embrace God's wonderful gift of salvation, we no longer need to pull out the legalism card to defend our personal preferences or distract from the real issues inside us. When we Christians are truly in relationship with Jesus, we desire to show our love to Him in any way we can!

> Greater love has no one than this, that one lay down his life for his friends. You are My friends if you do what I command you. No longer do I call you slaves, for the slave does not know what his master is doing; but I have called you friends, for all things that I have heard from My Father I have made known to you.
> —JOHN 15:13–15

We Christians keep the commands of God out of our great love for Him, not out of religious obligation. As Jesus revealed in John 15:15, He treats us as friends by keeping us in the loop, and He does it out of the depth of His relationship with the Father:

> So Jesus said, "When you lift up the Son of Man, then you will know that I am He, and I do nothing on My own initiative, but I speak these things as the Father taught Me. And He who sent Me is with Me; He has not left Me alone, for I always do the things that are pleasing to Him."
> —JOHN 8:28–29

Jesus continues to share with us the heart desires of Father God! He gives us insider information that is usually reserved for the closest of friends. The more we know Him and partake of the intimacy He offers, the more compelled we are to love Him.

Religion leaves you with a fear of breaking the rules, but religion in itself is not the problem. When we put our trust in traditions or rituals rather than the death, resurrection, and transforming power of Christ, we fall into a religious pit filled with fear. Jesus came to free us from fear, not enslave us to it. We come to Him through our conviction of sin and overwhelming gratitude for His unconditional love.

Sadly some believers misuse the grace Jesus lavished on us as a freedom to sin instead of freedom from sin.

Dictionary.com defines *religion* as "a set of beliefs concerning the cause, nature, and purpose of the universe, especially when considered as the creation of a superhuman agency or agencies, usually involving devotional and ritual observances, and often containing a moral code governing the conduct of human affairs."[8]

Living a life with Jesus brings freedom—freedom from fear-based religion, freedom from bondage, freedom from our selfish desires, and freedom to become who we really are! Sadly some believers misuse the grace Jesus lavished on us as a freedom to sin instead of freedom from sin.

In John 14:15 Jesus said, "If you love Me, you will keep My commandments." If we truly love Him, then out of that love we will do what Jesus says. Keeping His commands becomes a joy, not a burden. What Jesus spoke of in this verse is a clear way of measuring our love for Him. If we love Jesus, it will show in our obedience to Him and His commands.

Amazingly, however, we Christians often speak of love with

our words while speaking an even louder lack of love with our actions. We do not have the luxury of setting the level in this love for God; Jesus set that standard for us.

> In Him we have redemption through His blood, the forgiveness of our trespasses, according to the riches of His grace which He lavished on us. In all wisdom and insight He made known to us the mystery of His will, according to His kind intention which He purposed in Him.
> —EPHESIANS 1:7–9

Grace. I believe it is the most misunderstood word among Christians today. Too many in the body of Christ do not extend enough grace to the lost. Yet grace is used as an excuse by Christians to justify personal lifestyles and preferences. Grace is often regarded as the key that opens the door to a newfound "freedom" from authority to live out one's personal beliefs instead of aligning oneself with the complete Word of God.

The freedom Christ won for us is not without boundaries, as Paul explained: "You were called to freedom, brethren; only do not turn your freedom into an opportunity for the flesh, but through love serve one another" (Gal. 5:13).

If we allow it, love, grace, and accountability will work together to perfect us.

CHAPTER 4
GROWING COLD

Alcohol is the modern Delilah, bent on shearing the
church of its locks and robbing it of strength.
—DAVID WILKERSON

FRANTICALLY DIGGING THROUGH her purse as she walked into the house, Cindy was determined to answer her new cell phone this time. It embarrassed her when friends heard, "I'm sorry, but the person you called has a voice mailbox that has not been set up yet."

The caller ID displayed a familiar name and number. Joyce, the pastor's wife, had called several times in recent months. Ever since their grocery store encounter, finding an excuse to skip Sunday service had not been difficult for Cindy. She was not angry at Joyce or offended by her; on the contrary she admired Joyce in so many ways. If anything, she felt guilty for not answering Joyce's calls. She just wasn't ready to "face the music."

Before Cindy could find a good reason not to answer the call, she heard herself saying, "Hello?"

Joyce replied, "I sure miss you, girl!"

Her words made the conversation easier and more difficult all at the same time.

Inconvenient Realities

> At that time many will fall away and will betray one another and hate one another. Many false prophets will arise and will mislead many. Because lawlessness is increased, most people's love will grow cold. But the one who endures to the end, he will be saved.
>
> —MATTHEW 24:10–13

David Wilkerson understood this passage and was all but crucified by many in the church when his book *Sipping Saints* was released in 1978. The book was his reaction to a church culture filled with compromise. The message is as relevant today as it was then. Brother Wilkerson rightly understood our enemy spins webs and makes them seem attractive—so alluring in fact that God's people get re-entangled in nets they were freed from when they first came to Jesus.

We are quick to acknowledge that those who belong to the world use alcohol to numb life's many pains. Do we realize that as Jesus' followers we are not magically immune to seeking this numbing effect? Despite the scientific evidence concerning the influence of alcohol that has penetrated the mainstream media, some Christians still think the facts don't apply to them!

Christians who enjoy social drinking might be surprised to know that much of their sipping is actually making them legally intoxicated. For a woman such as Cindy who weighs one hundred twenty pounds, it can take only two twelve-ounce beers to meet or exceed the average state maximum of .08 percent blood alcohol while driving.[1]

Even one drink can make you an unsafe driver if it raises your blood alcohol concentration (BAC) to .08 percent or more. The bar is even lower if you're driving a commercial vehicle (.04 percent) or are under twenty-one years old (.01 percent).[2]

The following chart, used with permission from the California DMV, shows how many drinks it takes for a driver to become impaired based on gender and body weight. For the purpose of the illustration one drink is a 1.5-ounce shot of 80-proof liquor (even if it's mixed with nonalcoholic drinks), a 5-ounce glass of wine with 12 percent alcohol content, or 12 ounces of beer with a 5 percent alcohol content.[3] A person who has had fewer drinks could still be impaired if the individual had larger or stronger drinks, consumed the alcohol on an empty stomach, or had taken medication.[4]

BLOOD ALCOHOL CONTENT (BAC)
Table for Male (M) / Female (F)

Number of Drinks		Body Weight in Pounds								Driving Condition
		100	120	140	160	180	200	220	240	
0	M	.00	.00	.00	.00	.00	.00	.00	.00	Only Safe Driving Limit
	F	.00	.00	.00	.00	.00	.00	.00	.00	
1	M	.06	.05	.04	.04	.03	.03	.03	.02	Driving Skills Impaired
	F	.07	.06	.05	.04	.04	.03	.03	.03	
2	M	.12	.10	.09	.07	.07	.06	.05	.05	
	F	.13	.11	.09	.08	.07	.07	.06	.06	
3	M	.18	.15	.13	.11	.10	.09	.08	.07	
	F	.20	.17	.14	.12	.11	.10	.09	.08	Legally Intoxicated
4	M	.24	.20	.17	.15	.13	.12	.11	.10	
	F	.26	.22	.19	.17	.15	.13	.12	.11	
5	M	.30	.25	.21	.19	.17	.15	.14	.12	
	F	.33	.28	.24	.21	.18	.17	.15	.14	

Subtract 0.01% for each 40 minutes that lapse between drinks.
1 drink = 1.5 oz. 80 proof liquor, 12 oz. 5% beer, or 5 oz. 12% wine.
Fewer than 5 persons out of 100 will exceed these values.

Across the country you will likely find law enforcement and DMV officials in agreement about one thing: there is *no safe way* to drive while drinking. Cindy's home state says she is too drunk to drive after just two beers! Because a man like Jason has more body mass than Cindy, it will take him between three and four beers to hit the state's threshold of intoxication. What many consider to be safe and responsible social drinking is actually drunkenness according to the law!

Since the very beginning of my youth ministry in 1983 I have heard parents say these words countless times: "We would rather our children experiment with alcohol in our home than somewhere with people we don't know." One mother told me, "Better to drink at home than with people who could be a negative influence." And I always got a kick out of this one: "We are teaching our kids responsible drinking."

Well, Mom and Dad, how will you respond when you discover your state (a secular institution) holds to a higher standard than you do? What if the law says your child's responsible social drinking, which is supposedly in moderation, actually qualifies as drunkenness?

The moderation standard is tricky. You may have heard the axiom "What we do in moderation, our children will do in excess." There is wisdom in those words! And history has proven them to be painfully true. We need to look more closely at the word *moderation*, which means "the quality of being moderate; restraint; avoidance of extremes or excesses; temperance; the act of moderating." To do something, such as drink, *in moderation* means "without excess; moderately; temperately."[5]

A related word, *moderator*, refers to "a person or thing that moderates; a person who presides over a panel discussion on radio or television; ... a presiding officer, as at a public forum, a legislative body, or an ecclesiastical body in the Presbyterian Church."[6] It takes a moderator to administer the moderating.

A person can be a moderate, which is "a person who is moderate in opinion or opposed to extreme views and actions, especially in politics or religion; a member of a political party advocating moderate reform." The verb form of *moderate* means "to act as moderator; preside."[7]

The fundamental challenge with moderation is that the concept itself implies a moderator. History teaches us that we humans don't self-moderate very effectively, especially regarding issues like alcohol consumption. We need others to serve as moderators in our lives. It is a little embarrassing that we need to be moderated by a secular government. This is the inevitable result of the pride that we think keeps us "free" from the correction and direction of spiritual leaders.

Most states have adopted zero-tolerance laws that focus on drivers under the legal drinking age. For example, in Alaska persons between the ages of fourteen and twenty-one who are revealed to have "any alcohol concentration" in their blood are subject to penalty for operating a motor vehicle, aircraft, or watercraft.[8]

The fundamental challenge with moderation is that the concept itself implies a moderator.

In states with zero-tolerance laws just one beer disqualifies even responsible young people from driving. By this standard parents who introduce social or responsible drinking to their underage children are actually helping them reach a prosecutable state of drunkenness.

Moderately Drunk

I would propose that most Christians who drink socially are getting drunk without knowing it—at least according to government standards, which are often higher than those of believers. I think you get the point, but let's take a look at this from the scriptural perspective:

> Follow God's example, therefore, as dearly loved children and walk in the way of love, just as Christ loved us and gave himself up for us as a fragrant offering and sacrifice to God.
>
> But among you there must not be even a hint of sexual immorality, or of any kind of impurity, or of greed, because these are improper for God's holy people. Nor should there be obscenity, foolish talk or coarse joking, which are out of place, but rather thanksgiving. For of this you can be sure: No immoral, impure or greedy person—such a person is an idolater—has any inheritance in the kingdom of Christ and of God. Let no one deceive you with empty words, for because of such things God's wrath comes on those who are disobedient. Therefore do not be partners with them.
>
> For you were once darkness, but now you are light in the Lord. Live as children of light (for the fruit of the light consists in all goodness, righteousness and truth) and find out what pleases the Lord. Have nothing to do with the fruitless deeds of darkness, but rather expose them. It is shameful even to mention what the disobedient do in secret. But everything exposed by the light becomes visible—and everything that is illuminated becomes a light. This is why it is said: "Wake up, sleeper, rise from the dead, and Christ will shine on you."
>
> Be very careful, then, how you live—not as unwise but

as wise, making the most of every opportunity, because the days are evil. Therefore do not be foolish, but understand what the Lord's will is. Do not get drunk on wine, which leads to debauchery. Instead, be filled with the Spirit, speaking to one another with psalms, hymns, and songs from the Spirit. Sing and make music from your heart to the Lord, always giving thanks to God the Father for everything, in the name of our Lord Jesus Christ.

—EPHESIANS 5:1–20, NIV

The Spirit verse 18 encourages us to be filled with cannot be received by drinking. It does not come from a cup or bottle.

According to one organization, in the sixteenth century alcoholic beverages, which were used mostly for medicinal purposes, were referred to as "spirits."[9] The World Health Organization reports that 7.7 percent of the US population is alcohol dependent (25 million) and 13.9 percent have an alcohol use disorder (45 million).[10] The National Highway Traffic Safety Administration reports that "alcohol-impaired-driving fatalities accounted for 28 percent of all motor vehicle traffic fatalities in the United States in 2016."[11]

Statistics aside, the personal stories of former alcoholics all have one common denominator: they battled with demonic control or influence when drinking. But why would followers of Jesus allow any influence into their lives that has the potential to dominate them?

The Body Is the Lord's

The apostle Paul was clear about questionable influences, writing, "All things are lawful for me, but not all things are profitable. All things are lawful for me, but I will not be mastered by anything" (1 Cor. 6:12).

I am amazed at how aggressively some Christians defend what they love. I am not talking about evangelism or a command of Jesus but about personal preferences, habits, and worldly desires.

Test this for yourself: make a few posts on social media and watch the responses you get from Christians. I do it sometimes just to see where people are. For example, I'll post something about our freedom in Christ, implying that if we just add Jesus to our lifestyle, His grace will cover everything. Positive reactions, amens, and "thumbs ups" come rolling in! However, when I post a scripture about Christ's lordship, I get little or no response—it's practically ignored. If I dare to post about purity, personal sacrifice, godly living, or—God forbid!— holiness, you'd almost think I was threatening people's families!

Responses (or the lack thereof) from my Christian social network show that many are eager to engage in a verbal battle against what they see as overzealous and unrealistic ideas. The irony is that the same people who ignore some posts are quick to applaud posts with edgy movie quotes. The film's moral content seems to be of little concern to them because the movie was entertaining.

Pointing out any hypocrisy on these issues will get you even more convoluted replies, but nothing seems to trigger as much anger as warnings about alcohol. The very mention of a higher standard sparks outrage from some. Why are they so ready to defend the "innocence" of what I call well-marketed bottles full of decay?

If only this were not true of church leaders! I have personally watched leaders tolerate flimsy freedom arguments and defend their own right to drink. This in turn encourages their congregations and social media followers to take this so-called freedom to the next level, thereby introducing some to new numbing experiences and reintroducing others (who were previously delivered from their struggles in "Egypt") to painful bondages from the past.

I recall a certain pastor who reintroduced a staff member to social drinking. This young minister had previously been delivered, with the help of a faith-based rehab program, from many years of alcohol dependency. Unfortunately his new foray into social drinking led him back to his old addiction. In a short time he lost his ministry and his family.

The trouble went even deeper; the church was devastated by compromise among its younger followers. The domino effect was evident when several other young people returned to old lifestyles and addictions. Others who were introduced to this social moderation of spirits left the church and eventually walked away from the Lord.

> Whoever receives one such child in My name receives Me; *but whoever causes one of these little ones who believe in Me to stumble, it would be better for him to have a heavy millstone hung around his neck, and to be drowned in the depth of the sea.* Woe to the world because of its stumbling blocks! For it is inevitable that stumbling blocks come; but woe to that man through whom the stumbling block comes!
>
> —MATTHEW 18:5–7, EMPHASIS ADDED

Wow! Jesus' words are so very clear: stumbling blocks will come, but we must do all we can to make sure we aren't causing the stumbling.

Take a closer look at verse 6 from Matthew 18, which I italicized. The Greek word translated "believe" is *pisteuō*, which means "to think to be true, to be persuaded of, to credit, place confidence in...the thing believed [or]...a moral or religious reference."[12] Jesus does not specify an age range or physical time span but seems to refer to His young followers. The word translated "stumble" is the Greek word *skandalizō*, which means "to put a stumbling block or impediment in the way, upon which another may trip and fall...; to entice to sin; to cause a person to begin to distrust and desert one whom he ought to trust and obey; to cause to fall away."[13]

To the extent that we leaders avow personal tolerances that cause young believers (or anyone) to become re-enslaved in old sins, we become vessels used by the enemy. Although I would *never* tell Christians they are unsaved or living in sin because they choose to drink alcohol, I will tell them this: by using alcohol, you risk forfeiting huge opportunities to be used of God to bring transformation and healing to the lives of many.

Missed Opportunities

Let me give you an example: I often receive requests to pray for people seeking freedom from alcoholism. Do you think people trapped in this life-altering bondage would come to me for prayer if they thought I drank any amount of alcohol? I believe the answer is no. To them drinking is drinking, even if I drank socially and only on rare occasions. My level of consumption would be irrelevant because most people seeking deliverance started out drinking socially and in moderation.

Imagine for a moment that we are talking about marijuana and that you are hooked, smoking five joints a day. You are desperate for freedom from your costly, mind-altering habit. When you ask me for prayer, I say, "Sure, I'll pray for you. I only smoke a joint a week."

Do you still want me to pray for you?

If you are still game, how might these prayers of deliverance sound? "I command a reduced level of addiction in this person, in Jesus' name! Father God, reduce this out-of-control habit to a moderate one like mine!"

Feel better after that prayer? Does it seem compatible with Jesus' words in Luke chapter 4?

> The Spirit of the Lord is upon Me, because He anointed Me to preach the gospel to the poor. He has sent Me to proclaim release to the captives, and recovery of sight to the blind, to set free those who are oppressed.
>
> —LUKE 4:18

As Jesus stood in the synagogue to read from the prophet Isaiah, He knew the directive was not only for Him but for all who would follow Him. We as believers are also mandated to "proclaim release to the captives." Such public and private proclamations would have little strength if we were bound by the same spirits as the captives.

Allowing compromise to make us numb to God's laws is a treacherous path that leads to our love growing painfully cold.

———————— ◆ ————————

A few minutes after Joyce called, Cindy's phone rang again. It was Jason. She had conditioned herself for the "I'm meeting a client and will be home late" calls that had been increasing in frequency. Jason always said, "You have to invest in clients to see them invest in the company." Unfortunately these wine-and-dine "investments" were keeping Jason and Cindy apart—in fact much farther apart than she ever expected.

This was not what Cindy signed up for. Originally Jason opened his own computer software firm so they could spend more time together, traveling and enjoying life. Now her travel consisted of trips to the mall, the gym, the café, and then back to an empty house. It was becoming the very thing she despised about her parents' life together.

———————•———————

A new local café was one of Cindy's favorite stopping points and all the rage with young professionals. She enjoyed meeting friends there and knew it would be a comfortable setting for lunch with the pastor's wife, an invitation she had accepted by phone a week earlier.

The days since Joyce's call had passed too quickly, and now their meeting (which had made Cindy uneasy all week) had arrived. She pulled into the café parking lot early and knew exactly which table would best position her for a sudden exit if she needed it. Several conversation scenarios had played out in her mind during the drive over. What if Joyce asked about their drinking preferences? What if she asked why Jason and Cindy had been skipping services?

Hopefully there wouldn't be any personal questions. Cindy was not in the mood to get drilled today. Then again she was never in that mood.

———————•———————

Christians whose commitment to God is shallow tend to fear accountability and see it as an attack on their personal rights and freedom. You may have noticed that most people—Christians included—dislike being corrected and are quick to play the "Don't judge me" card. Many who claim to follow Christ resent almost any form of correction.

Obviously, welcoming correction is not exactly human nature. As a kid I had a wall poster of a large, scary-looking gorilla. The caption read, "When I want your opinion, I'll beat it out of you."

There is truth in a joke. We humans share the inherent belief that we can (and should) retain all control over our lives. This becomes problematic when we ask Jesus to be our Lord. The foundational desire to protect our freedom and remain in the driver's seat means we are choosing the title of *Lord* for ourselves and expecting Jesus to jump in when *we* think we need Him.

Stay with me here: Every time you drive a vehicle, you take control over it so you can influence its direction. Obviously, directing your vehicle is crucial to reaching your destination, which happens only by controlling the steering wheel and making corrections as the route demands.

Correction, direction, and control are also crucial to reaching the intended destination known as *your destiny*. Father God desires for us to surrender control over our lives so *He* can administer the correction that leads to direction and ultimately destination, which is destiny. Where we struggle the most is when God corrects us through other people, as He has done throughout recorded history. To this day He uses followers of Jesus to correct other followers of Jesus.

It would serve us well to examine and, if necessary, adjust our perspectives and culture where correction is concerned, recognizing its incalculable value to our well-being, individually and as a people.

Asleep in LA

I was just seventeen, driving through Los Angeles and pulling a camper trailer. Evidently I was not experienced enough for the job. As my very trusting father slept in the passenger seat, the sudden and alarming sound of tires running over the grooved portion of the freeway's right shoulder awakened him. He could see we were heading in a dangerous direction—off the road! He also discovered his son was sound asleep in the driver's seat.

With lightning speed my dad grabbed the steering wheel and corrected our direction just in time. After several over-corrections and despite my overall state of panic, our jack-knifing trailer steadied itself and we were once again heading safely northbound.

Like many corrections in life this one was not as painful as we originally thought it would be. Oh yes, my youthful pride was hurt, but the course adjustment was life-saving, so I ultimately embraced it. It's the same way when we Christians are corrected: we need to not only accept it but even *desire* it!

If we fear judgment, we have to ask ourselves what we are trying to hide. An innocent man standing before a just judge is not fearful. Instead he is eager to expose the truth and clear his name. Because our Judge *is* just, it is to our advantage to expose the truth even when we are guilty. We need to accept our missteps and own them. (Think how many past "crashes" might have been avoided if we had been open to correction and accountability.)

When believers say, "Don't judge me," they are really saying, "Don't correct me. Don't direct me. Just leave me alone." Their defensiveness is obvious when they say, "God alone is my Judge!"

Actually they are right. God is our Judge, but in His great wisdom He usually uses His sons and daughters to administer His judgment. Throughout the Old and New Testaments, Father God used His people to correct, direct, and judge His people. It is not the same for the lost. First Corinthians 5:12-13 shows us that Christians have no business judging the world or the lost. But as Paul says (and I paraphrase), "Are we not to judge the church, the body of Christ?"

Father God created us and knows us well. He knows we don't always listen to the Holy Spirit. Yes, we hopefully get better and better at hearing and obeying His voice (more on this in chapter 12); yet God knows we often need help from other believers to discern the corrective and directive voice of God.

Our Creator is so passionate about speaking to us that He does not even limit Himself to using people. We can be so thickheaded and stubborn that He has to correct us through donkeys, as He did with Balaam! (See Numbers 22.)

We really should stop asking the Lord to lead us if we are not prepared to follow whatever route and method He chooses. When we pray, "Be Lord of my life," are we not giving Him the full authority of His lordship over our past, present, and future? If so, then we should open our arms wide to embrace His life-saving, future-promoting correction, direction, and judgment.

If we truly desire the path God has for us, then we will also desire His way of training us, and we will recognize our place and purpose in His kingdom. Scripture says, "The LORD is a warrior; the LORD is His name" (Exod. 15:3). Not too long ago the church often referred to itself as "the Lord's army." We sang songs declaring it and equated discipleship with a form of military training and preparation. Through challenging prayer schedules, memorization of the written Word, and relational disciplines, the Christian lifestyle became like spiritual boot camp, equipping believers with the healing and power needed to take on demonic opposition, in the name of Jesus.

This should not surprise us. "The LORD is a warrior; the LORD is His name" (Exod. 15:3). One of the first descriptions of God we find in the Bible is *warrior*. Early Christians were ready to die for Christ and give their lives for the lost, motivated by the Warrior whose love for humankind and obedience to the Father carried Him to the cross.

Even Scripture speaks of us in military terms, saying, "No soldier in active service entangles himself in the affairs of everyday life, so that he may please the one who enlisted him as a soldier" (2 Tim. 2:4). A soldier in active service undergoes an intense style of learning designed to maximize his or her transformation in a short period of time. This process cannot be achieved without regular correction, direction, and judgment.

We need regular correction—everything from relatively mild orders to help us stay in our lane to more aggressive actions that awaken us from spiritual slumber when we are asleep at the wheel. Both minor and major corrections will come from others, inspired by the Holy Spirit to get us back on track with our destinies. Those who correct us have the same basic motivation my father had when he grabbed the steering wheel: they are more concerned with saving our lives and destinies than with coddling our feelings!

Run for the Gold!

No athlete has ever won a gold medal without relentless and aggressive guidance. Coaches necessarily give very pointed direction and frequently administer strict and necessary judgment. Athletes even pay big money for the intense guidance of a great coach.

Such guidance is often uncomfortable, but don't just allow it—desire it. Ask for it, and learn to love it! Correction saves us, gets us back on track, and builds our spiritual maturity.

Repentance is part of the correction process and postures us for promotion. A spirit of pride undermines our advancement;

it not only prevents us from receiving needed correction but also makes us afraid to covet it.

Do you fear input or judgment from others? Ask the Holy Spirit to reveal any walls you have erected against receiving the life such guidance promotes. Then repent of all resistance and rebellion so you might zealously desire godly correction like a spiritual athlete who is training to win the gold. If you do these things, you will enjoy traveling on your destiny road!

When we are consistently open to correction, it often comes as slight adjustments, much like the steering tweaks you make when driving your car. The type of harsh correction I received on the drive through LA is needed only when minor corrections are rejected or ignored. Believe me, I came to appreciate the scale of correction that disregarded my feelings in that critical moment. I am so grateful my father did whatever it took to keep us safely in our lane.

Repentance postures us for promotion.

If we are spiritually asleep at the wheel, we need and can expect aggressive correction. Spiritual sleepiness is a sign of a heart growing cold. Unless it is corrected, the heart becomes numb and unable to feel love, whether it is to be given or received.

Would you agree it is time for us as warriors of the cross to follow the life example of the One who enlisted us? Then let's receive whatever coaching we need, so we can win "the race that is set before us" (Heb. 12:1).

———————•———————

When Cindy arrived at the café, Joyce was already seated and motioning to get her attention. "She's like a trained spy," Cindy thought. "She read my mind and beat me at my own game."

Joyce stood to greet her with a hug that was a little longer than usual and somewhat disarming. The gauntlet had been thrown down, or so it seemed. Joyce bypassed the usual chit-chat and launched an opening statement of love and concern. It felt like a sucker punch that Cindy hadn't seen coming.

Joyce shared how Cindy had been on her heart and how she had been praying for her and Jason. Quite opposite of what Cindy expected, something inside her was released as Joyce spoke. She was not sure exactly what it was, but Joyce's voice calmed her. As the conversation continued, Cindy began letting down her guard. She did not even think about a new exit plan!

Joyce made no personal attacks but only expressed her concern. As she did, Cindy felt safe. She had always trusted and admired Joyce, but the safe feeling had reached a whole new level. Cindy thought, "Maybe Joyce isn't as overly religious as I thought."

The time flew by until they went their separate ways. Driving home, Cindy felt quite differently from how she felt driving to the café. The appointment went in the exact opposite direction of anything she had imagined. In fact she was looking forward to meeting Joyce again the following week.

That night when Jason came home late yet again, he was not interested in hearing about Cindy's day or her meeting with Joyce. Suddenly he reminded Cindy of her father. Life was becoming all about the money, and although Cindy had grown comfortable in their money-focused lifestyle, something inside her was shifting.

Money just wasn't enough anymore.

CHAPTER 5
HOLLYWOOD OR HOLY WORD?

If you were of the world, the world would love its own;
but because you are not of the world, but I chose you
out of the world, because of this the world hates you.
—JOHN 15:19

JASON AND CINDY'S Saturday night movie theater tradition became more of a girls' night out as Jason's business drew him out of town more frequently. This week, however, was special for Cindy because her husband was home. He picked the movie, and they settled into their favorite Saturday night spot—dead center seats—with plenty of popcorn on hand.

The night's feature was an action flick starring one of Jason's favorite actors. It was considered a must-see film, and everybody came out to see it. Jason even spotted a couple from church who walked in right before the film started and sat a few rows in front of them.

Fifteen minutes into the movie the church couple got up and walked out. Jason and Cindy could see the disappointment on their faces.

"Whatever," Jason said out loud.

On the drive home he told Cindy, "I guess some Christians

just can't handle the reality of life. They ran out like the film was X-rated! It's not like there was any total nudity. If it was because of the language—well, that's how people talk. What's the big deal?"

As they drove home, Cindy had a revelation: the couple that left never said a word to them, yet she suspected they saw her and Jason. They weren't judgmental; they simply left the building. So why was Jason so upset? And why was she feeling guilty? No one attacked them, but they felt judged. As it turned out, the real drama that night was not in the film but in their emotions!

Jason could not seem to let it go. "It was only rated R," he said. "They're adults, aren't they? So what's the problem?"

Jason made his point several more times over the next few days, trying hard to justify himself. Meanwhile Cindy could not shake the idea that maybe the other couple was right to exit the movie when they did. Perhaps she and Jason should have followed them out. She actually wanted to tell Jason the movie made her uncomfortable, but she said nothing. She knew his heart was set on seeing it.

———————•———————

The carnal mind rushes to see the latest blockbuster and then sits through inappropriate scenes, searching for something redeeming to make it seem OK. Why? And what exactly is the carnal mind? The definition of *carnal* offers some clues: "pertaining to or characterized by the flesh or the body, its passions and appetites; sensual: [as in] carnal pleasures" or "not spiritual; merely human; temporal; worldly: [as in] a man of secular, rather carnal, leanings."[1]

Another dictionary defines it similarly: "relating to the

physical and especially sexual appetites: [as in] carnal desire; worldly or earthly; temporal: [as in] the carnal world; of or relating to the body or flesh; bodily: [as in] carnal remains."[2]

Simply put, the carnal mind is worldly and nonspiritual in its nature. Yes, even Christians can be overcome by secularist leanings. That is why Paul urged us to pursue God's good and perfect will.

> Therefore I urge you, brethren, by the mercies of God, to present your bodies a living and holy sacrifice, acceptable to God, which is your spiritual service of worship. And do not be conformed to this world, but be transformed by the renewing of your mind, so that you may prove what the will of God is, that which is good and acceptable and perfect.
>
> —ROMANS 12:1–2

The word translated "urge" is the Greek word *parakaleō*, meaning "call for, summon; to address, speak to...instruction...to admonish, exhort; to beg...beseech."[3] The fact that Paul beseeched, called for, and summoned his brethren to be transformed by the renewing of their minds indicates there is a part we play in this process. It is not automatic; it results from the working out of our faith.

The idea of renewing our minds in Romans 12:2 is from the word *anakainōsis* in the Greek. This does not suggest a little tweaking around the margins of our mind-sets. Instead it means "a renewal, renovation, complete change for the better."[4]

One more thing about the passage from Romans 12—the admonishment "do not be conformed" is not a recommendation but a summons to proactively avoid worldly indoctrination. We must learn to filter out the attitudes and mind-sets that would conform us to the image of this world. To do this, we need look no further than the powerful written Word of God.

The Truth About Movie Ratings

When it comes to movie ratings, we have to ask ourselves: When did the Christian community start looking to the world for guidance about what to watch? And why would we hand over the job of establishing moral standards to a worldly, secular, Western culture?

Now for a little history lesson: Movie ratings can be traced back to 1907, when Chicago "became the first city to regulate and censor movies."[5] From that point through the 1920s other communities passed their own laws regarding acceptable film content.

In 1922 the movie industry established a system of self-regulation that is the foundation of today's ratings. That is when the Motion Picture Producers and Distributors of America (MPPDA) was formed. Its purpose was to develop and implement industry standards in the hopes of keeping cities, towns, and other government entities from censoring movie content. This was partly accomplished through the "Don't and Be Careful" list, which offered guidance to moviemakers.[6]

In 1930 members of the MPPDA adopted a specific code detailing standards for appropriate content. These guidelines were known as the Motion Picture Production Code, or more commonly the Hays Code, after MPPDA president William Hays. The following are examples of Hays Code criteria:[7]

- Films should not lower the moral standards of viewers.

- Audiences should never be encouraged to sympathize with violation of the law.

- Movies portraying criminal and adulterous behavior should show negative consequences.

- The law should not be ridiculed.

- Clergy should be portrayed in a positive light.

In 1945 the MPPDA changed its name to the Motion Picture Association of America (MPAA).[8] The organization and its members continued to use the Hays Code to guide moviemakers. As the social climate shifted in the 1960s and films reflected society's more "open" mind-set, the association felt pressured to update the code to reflect less stringent standards for acceptable film content. In 1968 the MPAA replaced the Hays Code with a new movie ratings system that removed restrictions regarding the types of content that could be included in movies.[9] This system gave filmmakers the ability to create whatever kinds of movies they wanted without censorship. The 1968 Movie Ratings System included four ratings:[10]

- G: general audiences (all ages admitted)

- M: mature audiences (all ages admitted but parental guidance suggested)

- R: restricted audiences (children under seventeen must be accompanied by a parent or guardian)

- X: no one under seventeen years of age admitted

Today's updated ratings system includes the following changes or additions:[11]

- The PG rating (parental guidance suggested) replaced the M rating. It suggests guidance for content that may be inappropriate for children.

- The PG-13 rating (parents strongly cautioned) was added to warn of content that may be inappropriate for children under the age of thirteen.

- The NC-17 rating (adults only) was formerly the X rating; viewers seventeen and under are not admitted.

How far we have come from the early days of the Hays Code!

How Are Movie Ratings Determined?

The MPAA does not actually rate movies. Assigning ratings is the responsibility of a board made up of an independent group of parents; the board is part of the Classification and Rating Administration (CARA), whose chair is selected by the chairperson of the MPAA with the agreement of the president of the National Association of Theatre Owners. Film producers and distributors who choose to participate in the movie rating system pay fees to have their films rated, and this money is used to cover CARA's operating expenses.[12] Participation is mandatory only for MPAA members, although the vast majority of filmmakers pay to have their films rated.[13] Board members view the films and assign ratings. Producers can appeal the rating if they disagree. (Appeals are heard by another board, two-thirds of which must vote to overturn a rating in order for it to be changed.[14])

Are you catching this? The body of Christ is submitting to standards created in Hollywood! There was a time when the church used the Bible as its standard of morality and then used that same standard to lead the nations in moral purity. My, have things changed! A small board of people (most of whose identities are unknown to the public) takes the lead over the church in matters of morality where film is concerned. Should they be deciding what is appropriate for you and your family—*really*?

It is disturbing to see the tailspin our culture is in—and I don't mean the world. Scripture told us that would happen. What is more disturbing is watching the church *following* the culture instead of *leading* it.

What Is NC-17?

The Dove Foundation, which was founded in 1991, approaches entertainment from a biblical perspective. Its former CEO (and one of its three founders), Dick Rolfe, describes one of the organization's early forays into how movie ratings work. It was a meeting with MPAA's then president, Jack Valenti, who created the 1968 rating system and was also responsible for the NC-17 rating initiated in 1990. In that meeting another of Dove's founders, Brad Curl, asked Valenti about the new rating:

> Jack replied that filmmakers were interested in releasing "edgy," "sophisticated" movies that were stronger in content than the current R-rating would permit. That prompted the next question, "Wouldn't those movies be rated 'X'?" "Yes," replied Jack. "And, since 'X' is equated with pornography, it would be impossible to distribute them through mainstream theater circuits."[15]

The pornography industry had already stigmatized the X rating. The NC-17 rating was a way around that problem. Yet according to Rolfe, "most NC-17 movies are so sexually explicit that they fall under the 'harmful to minors act' in most states," so much so that giving minors access to these films would be a prosecutable offense.[16]

Industry executives like Jack Valenti are not guided by moral absolutes but by the shifting tides of an increasingly corrupt culture. Jack Valenti admitted to Dick Rolfe that movie ratings are crafted to reflect society's *changing* values. Even CARA's chairperson, Joan Graves, confessed the rating system is elastic in order to reflect what becomes culturally acceptable over time. To make her point, Ms. Graves used the specific example of relaxed ratings for rough language. Why were these ratings relaxed? Because vulgar language is more broadly accepted in the culture.[17]

Many Christians have relaxed their views and developed a tolerance for what was once called *sin*.

She got that right, but whose culture is she talking about?

Unfortunately this is happening smack dab in the middle of Christian culture! Much like the MPAA, many Christians have relaxed their views and developed a tolerance for what was once called *sin*.

My point is not intended to start a witch hunt within the church. The issue here is with people who profess to align themselves with the teachings of Jesus but then live the teachings of a godless culture. This relaxing makes us spiritually lazy and unable to flex the muscles of our spiritual conviction. Much like King Ahab we have become comfortable with sin.

Jesus' words in Revelation 2:20 are very plain about relaxing God's mandates:

> But I have this against you, that you tolerate the woman Jezebel, who calls herself a prophetess, and she teaches and leads My bond-servants astray so that they commit acts of immorality and eat things sacrificed to idols.
>
> —REVELATION 2:20

Jesus put God's people in the "guilty basket" with King Ahab. They knew Jezebel was evil, yet they chose to tolerate her demonic influence over a nation. Please do not miss the implications of that judgment to us today. Don't many Christian parents allow Hollywood to decide which influences are or are not morally acceptable for their families? Are they not tolerating ungodliness?

Mel Gibson's *The Passion of the Christ* was rated R by the MPAA because of its graphic violence in depicting the death of Jesus. *Harry Potter and the Deathly Hallows* was "rated PG-13 for some sequences of intense action violence, frightening images and brief sensuality."[18] Are the violent images in *The Passion of the Christ* less moral or more damaging than images in *Harry Potter*? Which film is more spiritually beneficial to you or your children? Which is more aligned with scriptural living?

Many Western Christians (including Jason and Cindy) were raised to believe all G-rated films are safe, and Jesus *really* disapproves only of those nasty X-rated movies. If Christians used the "holy Word" standard of morality instead of the "Hollywood" standard, even some G-rated movies would be off-limits in their homes.

Instead millions of Christians conform themselves to the

world system and forget what God requires of them. His Word is crystal clear, however:

> When you enter the land the LORD your God is giving you, do not learn to imitate the detestable ways of the nations there. Let no one be found among you who sacrifices their son or daughter in the fire, who practices divination or sorcery, interprets omens, engages in witchcraft, or casts spells, or who is a medium or spiritist or who consults the dead. Anyone who does these things is detestable to the LORD; because of these same detestable practices the LORD your God will drive out those nations before you. You must be blameless before the LORD your God.
>
> —DEUTERONOMY 18:9–13, NIV

If I hadn't stepped on your toes to this point, I may have done it now! If we *lived* by these words from Scripture, movies such as *Aladdin*, *The Little Mermaid*, *Escape to Witch Mountain*, *Bedknobs and Broomsticks*, *Mary Poppins*, *Alice in Wonderland*, and the 1939 classic *The Wizard of Oz* (to name a few) would be eliminated from our collections. In fact we would purge *all* bewitching entertainment and education from our libraries.

These movies and so many other films, television programs, and cartoons have successfully taught "safe witchcraft" to an unassuming body of Christ. *The Wizard of Oz* introduced millions of children and families to the "good witch" concept, and G-rated films continue to desensitize families to occult practices by promoting witchcraft, magic, sorcery, mediums, and spiritists—and even instructing viewers in the art of casting spells!

I suppose most followers of Jesus would agree the R-rated

film *The Passion of the Christ* is a great benefit to families overall and to children old enough to understand the context of the violence. Yet according to CARA, a G-rated film glorifying witchcraft is safer for our children than an R-rated film about the suffering of Jesus!

Don't you think it's time we implemented our own rating system—the one found in the pages of the Book we as Jesus' followers once lived by?

CHAPTER 6
SEDUCED BY DECEPTION

Deliver my soul, O LORD, from lying
lips, from a deceitful tongue.
—PSALM 120:2

HER WEEKLY MEETING with Joyce was becoming the highlight in Cindy's life. Their first meeting left her feeling so surprisingly safe and secure that she enthusiastically agreed to meet with Joyce once a week in the same little café. Joyce's schedule was a bit more challenging than Cindy's, but between meetings their communication grew stronger via text messages.

After three months of getting together, their conversations gradually moved into deeper matters. Cindy initiated this by opening up about her past and present struggles. She was relieved Joyce had never brought up the alcohol issue. As far as Cindy was concerned, the subject was still one to be left alone. "People's opinions and convictions are their own business," Cindy thought.

Cindy's overall social life had not changed much, at least not outwardly. She still spent time with her friends, but she was becoming increasingly aware of how shallow these relationships were. Her friendship with Joyce had already become the maturest she had ever experienced.

As for Jason, business was flourishing, and he racked up more airline miles than ever. There were so many leads to pursue, and he wasn't about to let someone else turn them into new clients. His software company was turning great profits, but Jason still needed every connection he could muster. In addition to clients he needed investors to get his new line of wireless hardware up and running.

Jason's sales experience had come in handy, and his wine-and-dine entertaining was taking on a life of its own. His schmoozing surely wasn't hurting the firm's growth, but there was a catch: much the way the movie industry adjusts itself to oblige a more open-minded audience, Jason's standards about alcohol changed in direct correlation to his company's growth. So did his lifestyle.

Cindy was secretly concerned, but who was she to say anything? Yes, her own alcohol consumption was minor compared to Jason's, but she still drank, and she knew it compromised any leverage she had on the subject.

Slippery Slopes and "Light Bulb" Moments

Proverbs 12:1 tells us, "Whoever loves discipline loves knowledge, but he who hates reproof is stupid." Our discipline or lack thereof speaks loudly to others. It is nearly impossible to have a voice on issues we have not personally conquered.

Nobody had to tell Cindy that. She believed that if someone challenged her moderate drinking, they had better not be sipping themselves. This is exactly why Christians who drink (at any level or degree) are hesitant to confront Christians who are drinking too much. They know their ability to influence others is impaired because they have forfeited any real authority to speak on the subject.

It's common sense really. If your marriage is falling apart, do you seek guidance from someone whose marriage is also on the rocks or only slightly stronger than yours? No, not if you have a brain and are serious about getting marital help! Wisdom is found in seeking counsel from those who have gone through marital difficulties and successfully made it to the other side.

This is a natural human conclusion from the logical part of the brain our Creator gave us. It is the ability not to be stupid.

———◆———

Eleven a.m. calls were on the early side for this regular Saturday caller. Cindy answered with the best-sounding "Good morning, Mother" she could muster, despite her dwindling excitement for her mom's calls.

"Hello, sweetie. How did you know it was me?"

Cindy's mother had yet to grasp this caller ID stuff, yet she dominated the conversation as she usually did, ranting on and on about the injustices in her life. As she spoke, Cindy seemed to shrivel into a little girl. She hated it, yet she could not help but feel small around her mother.

Mom discussed all her past pains and some new ones. Her second marriage, which lasted only two years, had now become a reminder of her first (to Cindy's dad). Now Mom was blaming Dad for both marriages, and Cindy wished the call would end. Usually she motioned to Jason to call her or ring the doorbell—anything to end Mom's rant! But with Jason out of town her usual out was not an option.

After what felt like hours, Cindy agreed to meet her mother

at the mall, a shopping event they used to share weekly. On her way to the mall Cindy called Jason and got his voice mail again. "He must be with a client," she mumbled aloud.

Most days Cindy looked for any excuse to take a spin in the new BMW Jason surprised her with after his last extended business trip. The car made her feel good but not necessarily secure. Their life was changing, and troubling thoughts passed through her mind more and more frequently. "Is Jason really busy with clients?" she wondered. "Or is he seeing another woman?"

Cindy arrived to find her mom dressed to kill (at least her mom thought so). Cindy had always admired her mother's confident way of carrying herself. Lately, however, she was becoming less impressed and more irritated by it. Gina was in her late fifties and dressing younger than Cindy. A lift here, a tuck there, and all the other enhancements she'd invested in now drew long glances from men of all ages.

Gina had taught Cindy long ago that going to the mall was more about showing than shopping. As they browsed the stores, Gina paraded like a model on a catwalk. She made sure her physical presentation drew all the attention she craved. She then made comments about the men who gazed at her and responded to them in ways that seemed less playful and more blatant than ever.

Gina's tactics were nothing new, yet they bothered Cindy more than usual, as though she had begun to see them in a different light. As she drove away from the mall, she wondered, "Why are Mom's antics bothering me so much?"

Suddenly the proverbial light bulb turned on. "Mom did this even when she was married to Dad!"

Sure, Mom's displays became more overt after her first divorce, but it was obvious the motives driving her now had been in her heart way back then. Cindy began to recall the way her then-married mother flirted with other men. It didn't matter who it was—Dad's clients, the pool man, the UPS driver, the dryer repairman, and even the mailman! It was sport to Mom (acceptable in moderation of course).

Cindy remembered her dad's dislike for her mother's flirtatiousness and how Gina laughed it off saying, "Is Daddy getting jealous?"

Perhaps the demise of her parents' marriage was not all Dad's fault. Maybe he knew all along he never really had Mom's heart. Cindy doubted her mom would ever admit her part in the downfall of her marriage, but at least Cindy had a clearer perspective now.

Flirting, Flattery, and Seduction

Is flirting acceptable if it's in moderation? With flirting more common among Christians than we'd like to admit, the question is an important one. Like other practices, flirting has become part of our relational culture. Even if the intent is innocent, flirts operate in something much deeper. Let me explain and hopefully shed some light, beginning with a Scripture passage.

> For the commandment is a lamp, and the whole teaching
> [of the law] is light, and reproofs of discipline are the way
> of life, to keep you from the evil woman, from the *flat-*
> *tery* of the tongue of a loose woman. Lust not after her
> beauty in your heart, neither let her capture you with
> her eyelids. For on account of a harlot a man is brought
> to a piece of bread, and the adulteress stalks and snares
> [as with a hook] the precious life [of a man].
> —PROVERBS 6:23–26, AMPC, EMPHASIS ADDED

Insecurity creates an unhealthy desire in women to be wanted by men. Cindy's mother probably did not want to become an adulteress who stalks and snares, but her thought-less flirtations could produce the same results as intentional ones do.

The apostle Paul wrote, "As you well know, we never resorted either to words of flattery or to any cloak to conceal greedy motives or pretexts for gain, [as] God is our witness" (1 Thess. 2:5, AMPC). Paul understood the dangers and consequences of flattery. How I wish our young people understood it as he did. I, too, was very flirtatious as a young adult. It was an acceptable social play—yes, even within the church community!

Regardless of how safe and acceptable we think it is, flirting is hurting! That includes flattery, which is a form of flirting. I am not talking about the gracious compliments we give with no strings attached. The dictionary makes a very clear distinction between compliments and flirtation. A compliment is "an expression of praise, commendation, or admiration; a formal act or expression of civility, respect, or regard."[1] Flirtation is "the act or practice of flirting; coquetry; a love affair that is not serious."[2] Coquetry is not the gracious giving of compliments; it is "dalliance [or] trifling,"[3] which amounts to playing with people's feelings.

Love affairs that are not serious might sound like junior high school stuff. In reality adults are more seasoned in the method of manipulation known as *flirting*. It hurts people and can knock them off track spiritually. Playing with people's feelings through manipulation is a way of controlling their hearts.

Let's take a closer look at the meaning of the verb form of *flirt*. It means "to behave or act amorously without emotional commitment; toy or play with another's affections; dally; to deal playfully or carelessly (with something dangerous or serious); trifle; to think casually (about); toy (with)." The noun form of *flirt* is simply "a person who acts flirtatiously."[4]

Are you getting the picture? Flirtation ultimately leads to seduction, which is fueled by a self-focused heart that has little or no concern for the person being seduced. So let's talk about the word *seduce*. It means "to lead astray, as from duty, rectitude, or the like; corrupt; to persuade or induce to have sexual intercourse; to lead or draw away, as from principles, faith, or allegiance...to win over; attract; entice."[5]

The enemy wants to lure us away from our faith. In chapter 2 I compared media seduction to a spider that weaves a web of distraction, drawing us away from our faith and into a trap of faithlessness. Remember that the web is only the beginning of the attack. Next the spider poisons its prey. The seduction process is a poison to which the Westernized Christian is not immune.

According to *Collins English Dictionary*, a seducer is someone "who entices, allures, or seduces, [especially] one who entices another to engage in sexual intercourse."[6] We often use this word in relation to the seductress, a woman who seduces. Another term, *womanizer*, is also common in our vernacular. It refers to a male who seduces women. Colloquial synonyms for *womanizer* include "*Casanova, Don Juan, Romeo, gigolo, heart-breaker, ladies' man, lady-killer, lecher...lover-boy, rake, seducer, skirt chaser, stud, wolf.*"[7]

The womanizer is not generally applauded in our culture, but his initial flirting is often received with open arms. As for his female counterpart, we don't use the term *seductress* very much today. But the female seducer's advances also tend to be welcomed and are usually disguised in the cloak of seeming harmlessness. A seducer's wiles lead straight to the web where many people find themselves trapped.

By the way, synonyms for *seductress* include *jezebel, seducer, siren, temptress,* and *vamp.*[8] Did you catch that? Jezebel made

the thesaurus! This wife of King Ahab (her very name identi-
fies a spirit that seduces people inside and outside the church)
used her sexuality to manipulate power that was not hers.
That authority was not obtained in a sudden hostile takeover;
it was a slow, behind-the-scenes process of seduction empowered by witchcraft.

This is not a book about the Jezebel spirit. Others have
written about its workings against the church in much detail.
In his book *Unmasking the Jezebel Spirit* the late John Paul
Jackson enlightens us to the spirit's seductive methodology:

> Flattery is a primary tool used by someone influenced
> by the Jezebel spirit. Flattery is often used to pry open
> a door to endorsement by church leadership. Although
> offering sincere compliments that edify others in the
> Body of Christ are good, flattery differs in its motive.[9]

Manipulation is essential to Jezebel and all seducers, so
let's take a closer look at manipulation, which is "the act of
manipulating; the state or fact of being manipulated; skillful
or artful management."[10] According to the dictionary, *manipulate* means "to manage or influence skillfully, especially in
an unfair manner: [as in] to manipulate people's feelings; to
handle, manage, or use, especially with skill, in some process
of treatment or performance: [as in] to manipulate a large
tractor; to adapt or change (accounts, figures, etc.) to suit
one's purpose or advantage."[11]

Are you following the pattern? Flattery is a form of flirtation,
flirtation leads to manipulation, manipulation leads to seduction, and seduction is a work of witchcraft. The current Western
culture is certainly not void of such relational practices. Both
inside and outside the church these demonically influenced
social maneuvers are too often tolerated and even considered

acceptable. The proof is that many claiming to be followers of Jesus take offense when others teach or pursue purity.

Flirting is hurting sounds like an overreach to some, but is it? Ask the person with the broken marriage—the one who lost trust because of lust. Ask the children who watched their parents' relationship dissolve before their eyes. I doubt they would think the association between flirting and hurting is farfetched.

Cindy's mother's behavior was not random. She was driven by the insecurity, hurt, and loneliness that clouded her vision. Cindy knew her mom was not in the spiritual place to recognize her motives or receive correction, especially not from her own daughter. Cindy wished she could somehow convince her mom to own her part in the divorce and quit putting the entire blame on Cindy's dad.

Cindy felt as though her last encounter with her mom had triggered something in her own heart: a strong desire to have her dad back in her life. This was the same dad whom she had been warned against for so many years—the dad she was told "didn't give a rip" about her. Suddenly Cindy realized she had always harbored a deep desire to connect with her dad. She knew now that she wanted and needed a relationship with her father.

Stuck in Default Mode

Don't be surprised when those who once changed your dirty diapers resist your part in changing their hearts. Jesus understood this dynamic, not only in His divine wisdom but also from firsthand experience.

77

When Jesus had finished these parables, He departed from there. He came to His hometown and began teaching them in their synagogue, so that they were astonished, and said, "Where did this man get this wisdom and these miraculous powers? Is not this the carpenter's son? Is not His mother called Mary, and His brothers, James and Joseph and Simon and Judas? And His sisters, are they not all with us? Where then did this man get all these things?" And they took offense at Him. But Jesus said to them, "A prophet is not without honor except in his hometown and in his own household." And He did not do many miracles there because of their unbelief.

—MATTHEW 13:53–58

Jesus' lack of miracles did not reflect a lack of desire on His part. On the contrary Jesus saw the need, loved the people, and was ready to bring healing and transformation. They were not receptive, however. Their memories from the past became mental blocks. Relational familiarity kept them from seeing Jesus for who He really was.

Could it be God doesn't need our help in reaching our families? Maybe the best thing we can do is to pray for them, trusting Him to do the work. Perhaps in His divine wisdom and love Father God will send them someone who will effectively speak His healing words in a manner they can receive.

Cindy recognized her mother's need, just as we recognize certain needs in the lives of our loved ones. She loved her mother and wanted to speak truth into her life, but Gina was not open to Cindy's outreach. Maybe it was because she would forever see Cindy as her little girl—the one whose diaper needed to be changed by the parent and not the other way around.

The important thing is Cindy now recognized her mother's

seductive influence. It was obvious to her and no doubt to others. Yet her mother seemed completely blind to it. As far as Gina was concerned, it was exactly what successful communication with others (especially men!) looked like.

Cindy's mom is like millions of people who are influenced by seductive spirits. They sincerely believe flirtation is harmless. Of course some flirters are well aware of what they are doing and are fully intentional in using it. They know that flirting is hurting, but they use the social acceptability to facilitate and shield their manipulations.

Whatever the seducer's intent, the behavior stems from deeply embedded mind-sets. Much like the computers we use every day, we have default settings. Because these settings operate in the background, we need to ask ourselves, What are *my* default settings?

Until we identify these defaults, we will continue to be ruled by them. It is like Scripture says, "As a dog returns to his own vomit, so a fool repeats his folly" (Prov. 26:11, NKJV). Our default settings preprogram our responses. The programming is not random; it comes from our experiences in life, both good and bad. Left unchallenged, this programming continually draws us in the same direction, leading us either back to our past or into our future.

When we try to fill the empty spaces in our hearts, our wants govern our actions. If attention from the opposite gender makes us feel better about ourselves, we will relentlessly pursue that attention. On the other hand, if we realize what we really need is God's healing and deliverance, these needs will program our hearts.

Until our hearts are trained to believe God's truth about us, we will easily accept any lie from Satan, who is the father of all lies. Lie-based thinking comes from what he wants us to think about ourselves. Truth-based thinking comes from what God thinks of us. As we denounce the enemy's lies and embrace what God says, our needs and desires will be transformed into godly thoughts toward ourselves and those around us. When this happens, our hearts become loving and gracious toward others. Until we acknowledge Father God as our sole (soul) provider, we will continue searching for the people we think can fulfill our needs. (The plain truth is that no person can ever live up to such an assignment, so we end up reaping worse and worse results.)

Like Cindy's mother we are wired to feed our need. It is in our DNA and is seen from our first cries for our mother's milk. As we mature spiritually, we realize how much we need our heavenly Father. Then He does what only He can do: He feeds us physically, mentally, emotionally, and spiritually.

Yes, Jesus can and will fill your love tank and mine! When we recognize He is our provider, then we seek Him and He provides what we really need. Safely tucked in His love, we can admit that flirting is hurting, that lust breaks trust, and that love and forgiveness bring healing and restoration to broken lives.

CHAPTER 7
A FATHER'S LOVE

"I will be a father to you, and you shall be sons and daughters to Me," says the Lord Almighty.
—2 CORINTHIANS 6:18

"MR. WALTERS IS in a meeting. May I take a message?" the young, efficient-sounding receptionist asked.

It was not a surprise. Cindy's father had become more elusive in recent years and had not called her in more than twelve months. She wasn't offended by this. How could she be? She had taken her mother's side during and after the divorce and had not attempted to call her father. If the light bulb had not gone on while shopping with her mom recently, Cindy might not be calling him now.

Yet she was. Her thinking had undergone some changes. Perhaps she had judged her father too harshly all these years. Pushing him aside was not working for her anymore. Sure, her life looked good on the outside. Jason was successful in business, and they owned a nice home in an upper-middle-class neighborhood. Her new BMW seemed to profess Jason's love, and it gave her all the right feelings. But something was still missing in her life.

Maybe Dad had a part to play. She only knew she could not shake the deep-seated desire to see him and at least talk to him. No wonder her heart started pumping when she saw his number flashing on her phone.

"Daddy?" she asked softly. Calling him Daddy felt a little odd. She had not called him that in many years, but it felt good to her now.

Her dad seemed moved by her greeting too. "Hey, pumpkin," he said tenderly.

Cindy had not heard her father say that since before he moved out of the house. The phone call, however short-lived, was the best one she could remember having with him *ever*. They agreed to meet at their favorite breakfast diner (it was actually her dad's favorite place to eat). It had changed owners twice, but her dad was convinced they still served the best biscuits and gravy. For Cindy it was never about the food but about the time with Dad. The few times he took her there were permanently imprinted in her mind. Not that it mattered where they ate—she would be happy just being in her daddy's company.

She had longed for this throughout the years. She cried for it, planned for it, and even dreamed of having her dad's attention. Now, after so much had changed in both their lives, she felt the longing for her dad as she drove to the diner.

She spotted the familiar corner building from a block away. As she parked the Beemer, she was surprised by the level of nervous excitement she felt. It was the same excitement she felt when her daddy picked up his little girl for breakfast dates long, long ago.

Father Love

Cindy's inner need for a father is natural. It is in the DNA of every human being to desire a father's love. When a father's heart operates in a healthy manner, his love envelops his child in protection, security, and validation. That love empowers his child for promotion in life.

The apostle Paul apparently believed in the importance of a father's love.

> I do not write this to shame you, but to warn and counsel you as my beloved children. After all, though you should have ten thousand teachers (guides to direct you) in Christ, yet you do not have many fathers. For I became your father in Christ Jesus through the glad tidings (the Gospel). So I urge and implore you, be imitators of me. For this very cause I sent to you Timothy, who is my beloved and trustworthy child in the Lord, who will recall to your minds my methods of proceeding and course of conduct and way of life in Christ, such as I teach everywhere in each of the churches.
>
> —1 CORINTHIANS 4:14–17, AMPC

Paul understood the need for fathers and the lack of fathers.

You might agree the father role has lost much of its value over recent decades. The media often portrays dads in a negative light, in part because of the abuse and abandonment committed by many fathers in our generation. Their victims' sense of self-preservation and self-protection has swung the pendulum so far as to all but erase society's appreciation of fathers in the home.

Cindy probably thought she would have outgrown her need for her daddy by now. In reality outgrowing it would be unnatural. Father God desires us to want Him! He delights in our love for Him. Like us, He loves to be loved. We actually got that DNA from Him!

———————•———————

The décor at her father's favorite eatery was so different from what Cindy remembered, and the place seemed much smaller than it did when she was a kid. Yet none of that mattered when she saw her dad stand up from their table to greet her.

"Some things never change," she said to break the ice, looking at her watch to acknowledge she was late again and Daddy, as always, was early.

"It's never too late to change," he responded with a chuckle.

Cindy went for the easy conversation first: "How is business? Where are you living now?"—anything she could ask to keep him talking. She so enjoyed hearing his voice and was only beginning—as they talked, laughed, and reminisced—to understand how much she had missed him all this time.

The thirty-minute window her dad had set aside was interrupted an hour later by a call from his office. He had to go, but Cindy let him know how grateful she was for the time. Then she took the long way home to reflect on it.

It wasn't that home would be noisy or full of interruptions. The house was empty, and Jason not due back for two more days. The drive gave her something to do and a different place to think. By the time she pulled into the driveway, she realized she had been dealing with loneliness. Somehow reconnecting with her dad revealed it. How ironic it was; back when she and Jason first built the house, she craved alone time. Now it was what she feared most.

Cindy could not wait for Jason to come home. He had promised ahead of time that he would take a few days off, and she was ready! The house could get only so clean, and clean it was. She could barely wait to see him and share the excitement about her father.

Meanwhile her breakfast with her dad had stirred a mixture of emotions that needed sorting out. It so happened that she and Joyce had scheduled dinner for that night—the perfect night for girl time with a newfound friend. Better still, Cindy knew Joyce would actually listen to her, which helped Cindy's appreciation for their relationship grow even deeper, even as her other friendships seemed increasingly pointless.

When dinnertime came, Cindy had her plan in mind: she would grab the dinner bill, which she rarely got to do. As she and Joyce chatted, the realistic décor in the new Japanese hot spot made Cindy (who had never been to Japan) feel like she was there. It was impressive, and the conversation was going well. Joyce opened up about her own father/daughter background, which shed light on so many questions for Cindy.

The evening was perfect but not for long.

"Oh no!" Cindy thought as Pastor Keith appeared. She was so thrilled at the chance to talk about her father that she had forgotten Joyce's advance notice about Pastor joining them after his missions board meeting. His entrance rattled and even intimidated Cindy, especially when he sat next to his wife and directly across from Cindy.

"This little get-together is over," she thought to herself as Joyce, with her usual composure, brought her husband right into the conversation.

"Cindy was just talking about a reuniting breakfast with her father."

"Great! Just tell the whole world!" Cindy wanted to shout aloud.

Pastor looked Cindy in the eye and said, "You are really blessed, Cindy."

She was not sure where he was going with that statement.

He paused for a few seconds, which felt like minutes, and

then explained. "Just this week I prayed with a young man who lost his father some years ago. He never really knew his dad and was still dealing with the loss—not simply the loss of a father but the loss of a relationship he never had a chance to enjoy."

Pastor Keith paused again and looked down at the table. It was obvious he was tearing up, but he continued in a soft voice. "His story took me back to my own childhood. You see, the only memories I have of my father involved abuse and abandonment. My eighth birthday was an especially emotional event. I was both hurt and relieved: hurt that Dad had left us and relieved that he had left us. My father had been so physically and verbally abusive to me, my mother, and my two sisters that his departure gave us all a glimmer of hope."

Cindy was speechless. How does a person deal with that? She always thought her separation from her dad, much of which was self-inflicted, was the worst emotional issue anyone could go through. Now she was stunned by her pastor's story.

"I'm not sure where my dad lives or whether he is still alive," Pastor Keith said. "One thing Dad did well was to leave us. No confusion about that—he left, and we never heard from him again."

Joyce flashed a supportive smile.

"Shouldn't she look more sympathetic toward his painful past?" Cindy wondered.

As Pastor Keith continued with story after story, the smile on Joyce's face continued and seemed more impassioned.

"How confusing is that?" Cindy wondered. "Pastor is pouring out the awful details of his childhood, and his wife looks like they just won the lottery!"

The story made Cindy downright angry. One situation and one hospital visit connected to another, like a never-ending relay race with loved ones passing the baton of pain on and on and on.

And still Joyce watched with a glowing, growing joy.

Pastor Keith paused for a moment, and Cindy jumped in. She had sat still for this injustice long enough. "Why do you keep smiling?" she blurted out to Joyce.

Quickly Cindy covered her mouth, surprised at the words that leapt out of it.

Pastor and Joyce looked at each other and smiled. "I can answer that for you, Cindy," he responded, wearing the same smile as his wife. "It all started a few months before I first met Joyce."

He had Cindy's attention now! She was eager to hear the punch line that would explain their goofy smiles. She leaned into the table as Pastor Keith delivered his answer.

"As you have probably guessed, all this pain and abandonment from my father built up inside me over the years. I grew very bitter and unable to trust anyone, especially men in authority. Then my high school football coach dropped a stealth bomb on me. I had no idea that he was a strong Christian! I suppose he had to keep it on the down low since he worked in a public school. Anyway, he pulled me aside to correct one of my angry outbursts and told me that he had been praying for me."

Cindy thought she just might go crazy. Pastor Keith's story had her on the edge of her seat.

Bitterness and Root Issues

Bitterness is no small issue. It's not a phase you grow out of. On the contrary it plunges its roots deeper into the soil of your soul with each passing day. The Bible calls it a "bitter root." The New King James Version says it this way: "Looking carefully lest anyone fall short of the grace of God; lest any *root of bitterness* springing up cause trouble, and by this many become defiled" (Heb. 12:15, emphasis added).

The enemy will breach your security through your insecurity.

This root *system* cannot be pulled out, killed, or exterminated until the root *issue* is exposed and healed. Let me explain, using insecurity as an example. Insecure people struggle with forgiving others and tend to operate in self-preservation as a natural response to their feelings of inadequacy and insecurity. The problem does not end there, however, because insecurity sets them up for other offenses. Every time a new offense comes, the heart encumbered by insecurity grows even *more* bitter. No wonder Paul was inspired by the Holy Spirit to write these words:

> Do not grieve the Holy Spirit of God, by whom you were sealed for the day of redemption. Let all bitterness and wrath and anger and clamor and slander be put away from you, along with all malice. Be kind to one another, tender-hearted, forgiving each other, just as God in Christ also has forgiven you.
>
> —EPHESIANS 4:30–32

Bitterness and its root issues have a very high price tag. The enemy is not playing. He will use your root issues to wear you down. For example, the enemy will breach your security through your insecurity.

Being kind, forgiving, and tenderhearted is difficult for insecure people. Not only is it hard for them to forgive others, but it is even harder for them to forgive themselves. Sin is sin, and bitterness is a sin that festers in wounded hearts. They might not be thieves or murderers, but the descriptions that apply to other sinners still have bearing on them:

- "Their throat is an open grave, with their tongues they keep deceiving" (Rom. 3:13).

- "The poison of asps is under their lips" (Rom. 3:13).

- Their mouths are "full of cursing and bitterness" (Rom. 3:14).

- "Their feet are swift to shed blood" (Rom. 3:15).

These words might seem harsh, but they are meant to steer us clear of further pain. Bitterness is extremely destructive; a bitter heart cannot help but spew out cursing. You have heard it said that hurt people hurt people. It is just as Matthew 15:18 says: "The things that proceed out of the mouth come from the heart, and those defile the man."

Bitterness tastes just the way it sounds. You can smother it in honey, but the root is still nasty. Bitter can get better only through the healing power of transformation, which is graciously lavished on us by our heavenly Father.

———◆———

Cindy was hooked as Pastor Keith continued his story. "I could not erase from my memory that one sentence the coach dropped on me. A week later I just had to know why he was praying for me. I wanted to know what it meant because I was really confused."

"Tell me more," Cindy nearly said out loud.

"I waited until all the other guys cleared the practice field. Then I asked Coach what the deal was about this 'prayer stuff.'

He said he'd tell me if I met him at my favorite burger joint after school. What a smart man! He had me hook, line, and sinker. He messed me up over one statement, tickled me with curiosity, and then dangled an In-N-Out burger over my head!"

Cindy wondered if Pastor would ever get to the bottom line.

Recognizing her frustration, Pastor Keith said, "Hang in there, Cindy. I will answer your question—I promise."

"Not soon enough," she thought. Yet after a few more tales about Pastor Keith's coach she started to settle into his story.

"After a few months of hanging out with Coach and his family off the field, I realized he had been treating me like a son. I had never experienced that before, and I enjoyed it. By the end of my junior year I considered him a father—the only true father I had ever known.

"And then it happened. I had already opened up to him about my past, but I was about to go deep. He asked me if I wanted my childhood hurts to be healed. Without hesitation I told him I did.

"Coach, whom I still affectionately call Dad, began to tell me the greatest story of forgiveness ever told. I was so amazed that a totally innocent man would take the punishment for others and even forgive His killers! What a crazy love for people!"

Cindy could see Pastor Keith's amazement had never worn thin.

"After living with anger for so many years," he said, "I was ready to try anything. Plus I trusted Coach. He'd earned my trust with his time, patience...his love, support...and countless Double-Doubles from In-N-Out Burger."

Trust's Power

Trust is a powerful thing. Think about it: we don't naturally trust people we don't know. As children we are taught not to trust strangers because trust makes us vulnerable. We allow ourselves to become vulnerable only around those with whom we have history. Those are the people we learn to trust.

Too often that trust is broken. As Pastor Keith learned, broken trust can be restored only when it is renewed, sometimes by a person who had nothing to do with it being broken in the first place. Coach helped restore trust in a young man who had good reason *not* to trust anyone. Coach earned Keith's trust and gave him a reason to trust for the very first time. Therefore Keith let him get closer.

God used Coach to begin Keith's healing through a relational process that opened his heart. Coach showed himself faithful, a trait he had learned from Father God. This renewed Keith's trust in a man and soon swung open the door for Keith to trust God. Then when he trusted God, Keith opened himself to God's healing hand.

Our trust in God begins with trust in a person because we were created to be relational. Once Keith saw Coach had done right by him, he could believe maybe God would too! Coach was no preacher, counselor, or shrink. He was an ordinary man who wanted to make a difference in a young person's life. Men's meetings at his church had focused on the need for spiritual fathers. So Coach prayed God would use him to father the fatherless.

This is the very heart of Father God! That idea meant more to Coach than the information he had learned. It became a personal revelation that empowered him to develop a father's love for Keith—so much so that he came to consider Keith his true son.

Our current generation is in dire need of fathers—true men of God who will step into hurting lives and be God's instruments of lasting healing. In the hands of the Master Musician these instruments make beautiful music that cuts through cultural and other differences and brings people from all walks of life together.

We men don't need college degrees to accomplish this task. We need only willing hearts, hearing ears, and a love for the fatherless. Sitting down with young people and listening to their stories can be overwhelming: My father left. I've never met him. I've had three stepdads. My dad died. One of my mom's old boyfriends is my dad. My dad made me do bad things. My father hurt me. My father committed suicide.

The stories go on and on.

Every one of them makes me pray, "Lord, bring these young people fathers. Embrace them through willing men who will lead them to You. May they experience true healing encounters!"

Such encounters with Father God so often come through the hearts of willing men, men just like you and me. A generation of young people is crying out for a father's love and protection. They don't realize their hearts are longing for Father God's arms to hold them—a desire that is woven into every human being's DNA.

With Cindy focused only on his story, Pastor Keith motioned for the bill and then continued. "Learning to forgive my father was the key to my healing and freedom. I really had no idea how bound with unforgiveness I was. Bitterness was actually keeping me in a state of hopelessness. It was as though I couldn't move forward because of the hurt in my past."

As Pastor Keith spoke, Cindy thought about Jason, who was only seven years old when his father died of a heart attack.

Pastor Keith continued. "Giving my life to Jesus became a natural step because Coach lived a great example for me to follow. He was convinced I needed to go to a youth retreat his church was providing, so he paid my way. That retreat was a defining moment for me. That's where I discovered my life purpose and decided to let Jesus take the driver's seat."

CHAPTER 8

DESTINY ROAD

The path of the righteous is like the light of dawn, that shines brighter and brighter until the full day.
—PROVERBS 4:18

CINDY MENTALLY REPLAYED her dinner conversation with Pastor Keith and Joyce all the way home. "Wow," she thought, "Pastor Keith had a rough life!"

The disappointments in her own life now seemed minor by comparison. So did her sniping. She realized the man she and Jason critiqued week after week was a good man with real feelings and an amazing story.

The dinner that started out perfect had ended up being transformational. Only one thing was missing: Jason. Cindy was glad he would be home soon. She couldn't wait to talk his ear off.

Vision, Restraint, and Purpose

Purpose—what an undervalued word! Without purpose people die inside. Does that sound a bit over the top? Think about it. Purpose is the driving force that gets us up and out of bed each morning. Sure, the threat of getting fired gets us moving, but that's not purpose; that's fear and obligation. Only purpose lived out day by day leads us to our intended destinies.

People without vision perish. I didn't make that up—the Bible said it! Vision gives us purpose, and purpose keeps us fully alive. It is the drive we need to move forward. Proverbs 29:18 says it this way: "Where there is no vision, the people are *unrestrained*, but happy is he who keeps the law" (emphasis added).

To restrain is "to hold back from action; keep in check or under control; repress: [as in] to restrain one's temper." It also means "to limit or hamper the activity, growth, or effect of."[1] Some restraint is healthy, but some only hinders us. Proper restraint keeps the "ugly" from maturing within and limits the development of anger, malice, hatred, and fear. To be unrestrained in the context of Proverbs 29:18 is to live out of control.

The New King James Version translates the first part of Proverbs 29:18 this way: "Where there is no revelation, the people cast off restraint." In other words they open the door to all kinds of sin and its consequences. But when wisdom is operating in their lives, it restrains them from making harmful choices and reaping negative outcomes. Wisdom is critical because a lack of restraint ultimately leads to death.

The King James Version of Proverbs 29:18 might be more familiar to some readers, and it gets straight to the point: "Where there is no vision, the people perish: but he that keepeth the law, happy is he."

A lack of vision is a condition with grave consequences: the prognosis is to perish, and *perish* means just what you would think: "to die or be destroyed through violence, privation, etc.: [as in] to perish in an earthquake; to pass away or disappear...; to suffer destruction or ruin: [as in] valuable paintings perished in the fire; to suffer spiritual death: [as in] save us, lest we perish."[2]

Perish is not a word you want attached to your memory, especially not when it means spiritual death. You don't want any part of these synonyms for *perish*, either: "*be destroyed, be killed, be lost, bite the dust, break down, buy the farm, cease, check out, collapse, corrupt, croak, crumble, decease, decompose, demise, depart, disappear, disintegrate, end, expire, fall, give up the ghost, go, go under, kick the bucket, lose life, pass, pass away, pass on, rot, succumb, vanish, waste, wither.*"[3]

I think you get the point: we need vision! Not all vision is healthy, of course. Hitler had plenty of vision. His demonically induced purpose was genocide, proving that any vision can motivate action, however warped it might be. Therefore we need to ask ourselves, Did my vision come from God?

A God-designed vision runs deeper in passion, wider in influence, and higher in commitment than anything we could design for ourselves.

Freedom and Destiny

Just as Pastor Keith's trust of people was restored through his coach, Cindy was learning to trust through her new friendship with Joyce. As this trust grew in her heart, Cindy became less focused on her past and more interested in the future.

It is not uncommon for the past to keep people from their future. Even most Christians have not yet tapped into their destinies. Many are doing their own thing in life and asking God to bless it.

Some would ask, "Is that so bad?"

Well, let me answer that question with another one: Did Jesus follow His disciples, or did they follow Him?

Jesus never said, "Hey, Peter, can I follow you?"

Instead He told a professional fisherman, "Come follow Me."

Are you tempted to ask, "Where's the freedom in that?"

Then consider this: Jesus did not bind His twelve disciples with rules; He freed them with healing and empowerment! Jesus offered them genuine freedom to find their destiny road. He could have let them continue the way they were headed, but He knew there was a greater purpose awaiting them. Jesus was keenly aware of the potential they possessed but had never even imagined. It was kingdom potential, and as long as they remained in their visionless condition, that potential would never see the light of day.

———————•———————

Finally! Cindy was on her way to pick up Jason at the airport. It had been just two days since her dinner meeting with Joyce and Pastor Keith, and the pastor's life story still preoccupied her mind. She had also been reflecting on forgotten desires and some goals for the future. The plans she had long protected suddenly seemed so shallow and purposeless that she was rethinking everything.

"Maybe it's time to talk with Jason about our goals," she thought as she pulled up to the arrivals terminal.

Jason had been gone far too long and had promised to spend more time with her. So he planned a weekend getaway at their favorite bed-and-breakfast near the coast. Cindy was excited even to pack for the trip and more excited at the prospect of having a real conversation about their future. There was so much for them to catch up on. So many new feelings, ideas, and questions had been percolating in her heart, and their planned dinner would be the perfect time to share them.

Jason had reserved the perfect table: out on the deck with the best view of the ocean. The sun was setting and the ambience was romantic. "It doesn't get any better than this," Cindy thought.

Jason dominated the conversation, which was completely focused on the business and how it was growing. He talked about a bigger house, new cars, a golf club membership, properties, a new warehouse—the list went on and on.

As he talked about new contracts and large orders from prominent companies, Cindy became less enthusiastic about what she had been waiting to share. She even questioned the idea of mentioning her recent meetings with Joyce. "Bad timing," she thought. "Maybe tomorrow will be a better time to talk about it."

Then Jason popped the question, "What have you been up to?"

Her big chance found her. Everything she had originally wanted to share rushed to the tip of her tongue. The question was where to start.

She started with Joyce. Jason appeared to be pleased Cindy had found a good friend. Then she told him about her meeting with her father and about some of Pastor Keith's story. She explained how the pastor's testimony had affected her view of her dad. She hoped Jason would be as excited as she was about these developments, but he seemed not to be.

She was a little disappointed when he interrupted her story to order a drink. Jason had graduated from beer to hard liquor. To Cindy it was no longer about a particular drink. Alcohol now seemed symbolic of something larger in their lives. For Jason a cocktail represented success and freedom. For Cindy it represented a growing problem.

She could not take her eyes off Jason's glass. It was as though that drink would infect their entire destiny.

Dwarfed, Delayed, or Denied?

Can our choices affect our destinies? Absolutely!

For too many Christians the heart condition of compromise steers them away from biblical foundations and toward a kind of cultural correctness. This lifestyle is not benign; it will dwarf, delay, or even deny a person's heaven-designed destiny.

I am not talking here about destiny in terms of salvation. The point here is that because of their personal choices, many or even most followers of Jesus will never tap into the fullness of their life's design.

That statement has many weighty implications, so let's examine it more closely. I like pie charts (not as much as I'd like a slice of pie, but I digress). If there were a pie chart representing the destinies that have been dwarfed, delayed, or denied, I believe dwarfed destinies would be the largest slice. Delayed destinies would be the next largest, and denied destinies would be the smallest slice, as pictured below.

Now let's talk about all three, maybe while you grab a slice of pie and a cup of joe.

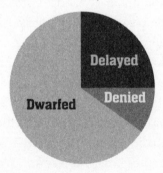

Dwarfed Destiny

Living in perfection is not the focus here. This is about maximizing our respective journeys by following the voice and direction of Father God to the very best of our ability. If we manage to fulfill 75 percent of our created purpose, then our destiny has been dwarfed, which means it is "smaller than the average...stunted."[4]

Some life choices take us off our destiny road and onto a detour. Whether or not we realize the switch, we risk forfeiting a measure of our purpose, which can in turn dwarf our destiny overall.

Delayed Destiny

Delayed destinies are probably more common than we realize. I can certainly confess my destiny was delayed by my selfish decisions and overall procrastination concerning God's direction for my life.

Because of our heavenly Father's grace and restoration power our eventual obedience can be maximized. But can we ever know how many lives went untouched during our self-centered pursuits? Will we ever know how many blessings we missed? It is on the journey that we **Procrastination kills destination.** encounter divine appointments, relationships, opportunities, and the potential to say, "Follow me as I follow Christ." On the journey (and especially on those self-focused rabbit trails) we need to consider the example we are setting for others. We need to recognize that people are following us, even when we are lost.

I would say that most delayed destinies are caused when we rebel against the call of God on our lives. Daniel Baker of Restoration Ministries once told me, "Procrastination kills destination."

Throughout this book I have given you key dictionary definitions, not as lessons in the English language but as opportunities to think more carefully and to locate yourself more accurately. The following is the definition of *procrastinate*.

Please don't skim it—this is powerful stuff. *Procrastinate* means "to defer action; delay: [as in] to procrastinate until an opportunity is lost; to put off till another day or time."[5]

Procrastination is costly! It causes us to miss opportunities, even the opportunities we have long prayed for! At the very least procrastination can significantly delay destiny.

Denied Destiny

In our context here *denied destiny* does not imply the loss of one's heavenly eternity. Take a look at the conversation between the thief and Jesus as they hung on their respective crosses: "[The thief] was saying, 'Jesus, remember me when You come in Your kingdom!' And [Jesus] said to him, 'Truly I say to you, today you shall be with Me in Paradise'" (Luke 23:42–43).

I doubt very much the thief had reached his full potential in life. Hanging on a cross might have been part of Jesus' destiny, but I doubt it was the thief's. We see in verse 43 that he went to heaven with Jesus, which is wonderful. But how had his life choices pulled him off his destiny road and toward being disgraced and crucified?

Because of the thief's rebellion his destiny in this life was denied. Thanks to the awesome grace of God, he was of course forgiven, and his eternity was redirected in the nick of time. Ask yourself this, however: How many people might have followed Jesus if this man had followed Him *before* he met his end? I wonder what kind of legacy he might have left behind if he had simply lived in obedience to God.

Carnality taints the fabric of our future.

Compromise seems justified for those walking the path of carnal thinking. It is a comfortable route; the enemy and everyone in his demonic realm find it inviting and try to make it inviting to us. The enemy's fondness for it makes sense, "for to be carnally minded is death, but to be spiritually minded is life and peace" (Rom. 8:6, NKJV).

Are you getting this? Carnal thinking brings death and spiritual thinking brings life! Maybe you have heard the statement "They are so heavenly minded that they are no earthly good." Actually that is a lie planted by the devil himself. The truth is that we are of little good to this earth unless our thoughts are heavenly and we are spiritually minded.

The enemy has easy access to those who travel the road of carnality. He feeds on those whose hearts and minds are bent toward fleshly ways. They are the ones he manipulates and infects. Satan knows that a mind occupied with the things of the Spirit easily recognizes his deception. However, he has little trouble breaching the seeming security of Christians who are tolerant of sin or prone to justifying it. Gaining control of their carnal hearts is easy.

Keep Covered

"Things will slow down soon and we'll have some time together." Cindy had heard Jason say it before, but she no longer believed it would come true.

She had married her best friend, but his new bestie was his company. So she kept busy with shopping, visits to the gym, and time with Joyce. Their girl times were becoming more important to Cindy every week. She even noticed that after each meeting her understanding of spiritual things seemed to expand. Many issues were becoming clearer to her, as though she was becoming smarter about life itself.

"I can meet you at the café on my way home from the gym tomorrow!" she told Joyce as they concluded their short phone call.

The gym had always been a priority for Cindy. Now with

Jason absent much of the time, her visits became more frequent. Apparently it was having an impact on her appearance. Hearing people say, "You're looking really hot, girl!" was becoming common, especially with Sam, a personal trainer who took a real interest in her workout routine.

Cindy appreciated Sam's expertise and often thanked him for it. This time when she said, "Thanks, Sam," something felt different. She enjoyed saying it and even felt a strangely pleasant twang of guilt—enough to keep thoughts of Sam whirling in her head on the way to see Joyce.

"How was your workout?" Joyce asked right off the bat.

"That's weird," Cindy thought. "Joyce never asks about my workouts."

Cindy lowered her eyes and said, "It went just fine. Thanks."

Cindy noticed a slight change in Joyce's expression. "Is there something on your heart, girl? Maybe something that seems insignificant?" Joyce asked.

"Wow, is she getting in my head or what?" Cindy wondered silently. She knew Joyce was perceptive. She also trusted Joyce enough to think, "Why not just talk about it?"

So she did. "I feel guilty! On the way here I couldn't get Sam out of my head."

Cindy shared every detail and every compliment Sam had given her and how she responded. She told Joyce how she felt about each encounter and laid bare her intentions and past flirtations. She even told Joyce where she got flirting skills: from her expert trainer, her mother.

Joyce sat patiently and listened. Then just as Joyce began to share some insights on the matter, a text popped up on Cindy's phone.

"It was really great to see you today, Cindy!" The text from

Sam was nothing new, but the heart emojis at the end were becoming more numerous with each message.

"Wow, his timing is crazy!" Cindy said to Joyce, handing her the phone so she wouldn't have to read the message aloud. Joyce scanned through Cindy's many texts with Sam and saw how the conversations had evolved. In a matter of weeks they changed from professional to personal—not all at once but gradually over time.

Joyce handed back the phone and reached for her latte. Before she said a word, Cindy asked, "How should I respond to him? What should I say?"

With her hands cupped around her coffee and holding it close to her chin, Joyce calmly replied, "Before I answer that question, let's get to the root of this."

Cindy's eyes said, "Yes, let's."

"Would you say that, just maybe, your heart is open to receiving comfort, love, or attention from someone other than Jason? Because if any part of your mind has broken covenant with your husband, then your heart will follow. So before I can help you with a response to this encounter, we need to expose the cause."

———————•———————

Joyce was experienced enough to know these encounters don't just happen. The heart does not open itself that quickly. There is a process and a conditioning that must take place first. Then over time they steer the heart in a new direction, from one posture to another.

If Father God has been denied the opportunity to fill any empty area of the heart, that chasm will drive us, whether consciously or subconsciously, to look for something or someone to fill it. What we often fail to realize is that no one, not even a spouse, can fill all of our empty places. The only one who can do that is the One who made the heart—God.

The heart is a funny thing. It tends to move toward whatever seems to feed it. Like babies being nourished by their mothers, we cling tightly to our sources of emotional input. Parents and spouses play a very important part in the growth and development of our hearts. Both can help us to mature so we are capable of receiving and giving love. Yet until we recognize Jesus as our primary and foundational source, we remain vulnerable to the inappropriate invitations that seem to satisfy our emptiness.

Cindy openly received Sam's flattery because his words and attention were feeding a need. Whether or not Cindy was aware she had this need did not matter. Her inner search for "filler" was actively at work. Some people are keenly aware of their emptiness and knowingly seek out attention. Others simply receive a "feeding" when it comes their way, unaware an empty heart has driven them to crave it.

The simple reality is this: when the love of Father God is not recognized as our first and final source, we are susceptible to the enemy's schemes. Of course Sam was not Cindy's enemy. He was not even the problem. There will always be predators looking for another adventure. The problem was in Cindy's own heart.

A heart starved for the love of Jesus is an effective gateway for the enemy.

———————•———————

The more Joyce talked about Cindy's encounter with Sam, the deeper the revelation went in Cindy's heart. It was as though her eyes were being opened for the first time. There was a sense of relief at having the enemy's scheme exposed, but even greater feelings of guilt and remorse began to overwhelm her.

Joyce expected this common response.

"Cindy, you and Jason have a destiny designed by God Himself," Joyce said. "The enemy is afraid that you might discover what it is and chase after it!

"See, the devil is truly afraid of those who travel their destiny road. He looks for weaknesses to exploit and has no problem finding people to distract us on his behalf. First he wants to draw us away from our covenant relationship with God. Then he can compromise the marriage covenant.

"That's why Father God so wants to be your rock, your foundation, and your source. He knows that even people in the very best relationships will let each other down from time to time. But He promised that He would never leave nor forsake us.

"When God is your rock, you can stay strongly in love with Jason, even when he is absent."

Tears streamed down Cindy's face. Her heart was beginning to break, not in a negative or condemning way but with a sweet conviction that cracked it open to the love she craved. The danger of her secret thoughts about men like Sam was coming into clear view. What she once saw as fun and safe fantasies now looked quite dangerous. She could see where they would lead—not in her mind but in real life. Her thoughts of sexual playfulness would have become damaging sexual realities.

The implications began to hit her. "The very thing I feared Jason would do was growing in my own heart," she whispered to Joyce. "That would have happened. I would have cheated. It was in me, and now these texts really make me sick!"

Sam sent another text. Cindy looked at her phone and then at Joyce. "OK. What do I say? How do I stop this?"

Joyce had been down this road with others and was well

prepared to respond. "The answer is simple, Cindy. Just put a third party in the loop, preferably your husband, as he is your marital covering."

Cindy looked quizzical.

"Think about it. Would Sam be speaking so personally to you if Jason was at your side in the gym?"

Joyce had Cindy's attention.

"I'm sure Jason would have something to say about Sam's detailed compliments of your body, don't you think?"

Cindy couldn't argue with that. As Joyce spoke, the scenarios of what Jason might do boggled her mind.

"If you found similar texts from another woman on Jason's phone, would that bother you? It sure would bother me if I found out Keith was receiving messages like that."

Cindy thought for a minute and then asked, "How do you know he isn't?"

Joyce was prepared to answer. "It's the third-party rule. If I have to send a text, email, or any other type of communication to a man other than my husband, I simply add Keith to the message. I cc him on everything, and if he is not available, I third-party someone else I can trust to point out anything inappropriate.

"Think about it, Cindy. This is common practice among professionals. A CEO will often copy one or more people on his or her emails for three main reasons: clarity, liability, and accountability. It keeps the conversation clear and to the point; it covers both parties legally; and it creates additional records to ensure understanding and accuracy. The third-party rule keeps 'he said, she said' issues from rearing their ugly heads."

Joyce ordered more coffee, giving Cindy a moment to take it all in.

Cindy's mind raced at warp speed as she flipped through old texts. She remembered long talks with other men and how good they made her feel. Her once-hidden motives were now exposed to a newfound truth.

Real freedom was developing in Cindy's heart.

———————◆———————

The enemy is fearful that we will find our destiny road and begin to enjoy the journey. One of his best strategies is to undermine relationships with secrets. The hidden areas of our lives are fertile ground in which he can plant and feed lies that lead to pain and our eventual destruction.

Our personal preferences—the things that help us to feel good—are more comfortable in the short term than the plain truth is. But our comfort zones leave little room for us to trust God with our destinies. Like people hiking through unfamiliar territory, we don't know everything that is ahead. However, if we know we are on the right trail, we can move ahead confidently, trusting that the journey, even with its many challenges, will be well worth it.

The enemy is fearful that we will find our destiny road and begin to enjoy the journey.

We find that right path when we recognize our purpose and weed out distractions. With that information under our belts the enemy's fog of confusion and doubt can do little to draw us away from the Father's plan.

CHAPTER 9
THE LIE OF INDEPENDENCE

Trust in the LORD with all your heart and do not lean on your own understanding. In all your ways acknowledge Him, and He will make your paths straight.
—Proverbs 3:5–6

JASON'S NEW PRODUCT line opened the way to more business in more places. This trip to Singapore was his third out of the country, and it produced a major contract. The host firm certainly knew the fine art of wining and dining, so it was no wonder Jason awakened in his hotel room dazed, confused, and stumbling toward the shower.

Jason quickly realized he had slept through his alarm. Unless he hustled, he would miss his flight home.

Fortunately he made it, but just barely. "That was close," he muttered under his breath as he dropped into his first-class seat. He made the flight only because it had been delayed, and he knew oversleeping was not the real issue. He had a bigger problem, one he'd become aware of months earlier. He just couldn't come to terms with confessing it to anyone, especially not Cindy. He was strong and would work through it on his own.

Or so he thought.

Although exhausted and still under the sway of alcohol, Jason actively ran through scenarios of recent close calls, mentally counting the many opportunities he'd had to compromise his beliefs and his marriage.

Having lost his dad when he was only seven, Jason held onto the positive memory of his dad's faithfulness. His mom had always spoken of how his dad would not even look at another woman. Maybe his dad was a bit old school, but no one could question his marital commitment.

Jason admired that and took his own marriage seriously largely because of it. As he sipped a fresh cup of coffee, he remembered how close he came to blowing it on this last business trip. Remaining functionally aware after several potent cocktails was not his strong suit, and on this trip Jason had consumed more than his limit.

It happened during a corporate gathering of more than a dozen business associates and clients in a large hotel suite. The atmosphere was businesslike but relaxed, and Jason's conversation with a new marketing associate started in an entirely appropriate manner. With alcohol blurring the lines, however, the exchange became personal. The marketing associate had left the fashion industry and entered the software marketing field. Her qualifications as a model were still obvious and quite captivating. Jason noted her good looks and enjoyed her accent, but he also tried to keep the conversation professional. Eventually, however, he realized everyone else had gone. He was alone in a deluxe suite with a former fashion model.

As she talked, something felt completely wrong to Jason. He could not help but run hypotheticals through his mind: What if Cindy could see this? What would it look like to her? What if this woman really likes me (which I think she does)?

What would happen if I stayed? What's the big deal anyway? We're grown adults.

The questions played like videos in Jason's mind. He watched them intently as he listened to the woman speak. Then his stream of consciousness was interrupted by words that jumped out at him.

"It appears that you have me all to yourself, Jason. We could get to know each other a little better if you like," she said suggestively.

"Did she just say that?" Jason wondered as he felt on the one hand a strong desire to stay and on the other an equally powerful urge to run.

She left him to his thoughts and crossed over to the bar for another round. It was clear to Jason where this was heading. He found himself grabbing his leather satchel and darting toward the door.

"Nice meeting you," he said awkwardly. "I need to get going."

Those were Jason's parting words. He never was one for long goodbyes, and he distrusted his strength to say no. In a virtual cold sweat he sped down the hallway and into an elevator, immediately hitting the button to close the door. Safe inside he pulled out the woman's business card, literally shaking as he glanced at her photograph. He crumpled the card, tossed it in the trash, and checked out of the hotel a day early. He knew he could not trust himself with her contact information or with this attraction.

Because of his burgeoning business Jason's pattern had been to arrive home a day or two later than planned. But this encounter had been too close for comfort. His best shot at averting marital disaster was to get home early.

"I Got This"

Having counseled many couples over the years, my wife and I find a common thread in every marital failure: "I thought I could handle it."

One of the enemy's favorite lies is that we don't need help.

In ministry we have seen this mind-set in every level of relational decay. It postures the heart to accept decay and through a false sense of strength sets up the heart to fail. The deception puts people in compromising situations that seem safe in the moment. Later, when they find moments of clarity, step back, and assess the bigger picture, they recognize their need for accountability.

This is what happened to Jason. He escaped danger this time because he responded to the right voice rather than the wrong one. But it was a coin flip that could have gone either way, and Jason knew it.

Our culture has softened the impact of words like *fornication*, *adultery*, and *infidelity*. The idea of breaking a marriage covenant is not the big deal it used to be. Acts of adultery and infidelity have been reduced to euphemisms such as "I'm having an affair" or "It's just a little hanky-panky." Cheating is widely accepted in our Western culture. Politicians cheat, students cheat on tests, and even some pastors cheat on their taxes.

Notwithstanding the softening of morals, fornication, adultery, and infidelity are serious and damaging breaches. For clarity's sake let's take a fresh look at these loaded terms.

Fornication

Many people see *fornication* as an outdated word—an anachronism that does not apply in our times. However, the word describes acts that are perhaps more common in modernity. Here's how the dictionary defines *fornication*: "voluntary sexual intercourse between two unmarried persons or two persons not married to each other; [in the] Bible, idolatry."[1]

The first part of the definition speaks to intimate relations that are premarital and therefore not sanctioned by the union of marriage. The second part speaks to spiritual fornication, which underlies all sin.

Adultery

This word is still in use but is often treated with less gravity than in past generations. It is defined as "voluntary sexual intercourse between a married person and someone other than his or her lawful spouse."[2] This involves the breaking of the marriage covenant. The word *voluntary* is used in the definition to exclude outside-of-marriage sex forced upon rape victims who are married to someone other than the rapist.

Infidelity

This word has broad application to many behaviors and is largely used to describe marital breaches. *Infidelity* includes "marital disloyalty; adultery; unfaithfulness; disloyalty; lack of religious faith, especially Christian faith; a breach of trust or a disloyal act; transgression."[3]

In the context of marriage, infidelity is the absence of "conjugal faithfulness."[4] The act of adultery is fundamentally an act of disloyalty, which breaks trust in a relationship. Disloyalty, however, is established in the heart long before it manifests in a physical act. Infidelity can be nipped in the bud through accountability, which protects those who are tempted.

The definition of *accountability* is simple: "the state of being accountable, liable, or answerable; [in] education, a policy of holding schools and teachers accountable for students' academic progress by linking such progress with funding for salaries, maintenance, etc."[5]

The nature of today's culture is at odds with the very idea of accountability. Our school systems are designed to indoctrinate students (in the name of education), molding the minds and values of successive generations and teaching them to self-define morality. In the prevalent absence of moral and spiritual absolutes the thought of one person holding another person accountable seems archaic.

When the pain of adultery becomes real, those who once resisted accountability (yes, I *am* talking about Christians) ask the usual questions: How did this happen? Could I have stopped it from happening? Had they embraced accountability ahead of the crisis, these questions would not need to be asked. But because they valued individual independence over accountability, the best they can do is swallow their pride and submit to accountability *after* the damage is done, counseling sessions have begun, and support meetings are underway. What they realized too late would have kept them wonderfully protected early on.

The nature of today's culture is at odds with the very idea of accountability.

———•———

Jason's in-flight power nap was not the result of his hard work in building a business. It was more like an alcohol-induced coma. When he awakened, he was disoriented and wondered briefly where he was. As was his practice when in this condition, he asked for another coffee and then another.

After several cups Jason's mind cleared. Had he needed his mind for business, he could have summoned it. He was strongly conditioned to focus on success and the growth of his company. What he needed now was not his aptitude for numbers, net worth, or the bottom line; he needed to think about life itself, which was far less cut and dried.

He mumbled to himself, "What is all this for?"

The man sitting next to him noticed Jason's stirring. When Jason boarded the flight, the man seemed engrossed in a book, so Jason had not connected with him. Now the man broke the ice.

"That was quite a rest you just had. Apparently you have been working too hard." The man leaned in toward Jason as he spoke.

"Oh yeah. Well, that comes with the territory, I guess," Jason replied.

The man handed Jason his business card, and Jason reciprocated.

"I would imagine the continual advancements in electronics must keep a young man like you on your toes," Frank Benson said as he examined Jason's business card.

He continued asking Jason about his company and the many facets of the electronics industry. The subject was Jason's passion, so it didn't take him long to fully engage in the conversation. The men talked for more than two hours, but Jason felt comfortable within the first few minutes. The older man was soft-spoken but without appearing slack or weak in any way. His eyes were compassionate yet piercing; his overall persona was that of a loving father.

As Mr. Benson talked about family, Jason realized he had tucked away the man's business card without noticing his occupation. Now he discreetly pulled it out and read the bold, raised letters: "Life Coach, Frank S. Benson." A separate line said, "Coffee Expert: making a difference, one cup at a time." In smaller print at the bottom of the card there was a Scripture reference: Psalm 139:13–14.

Frank seemed safe, and Jason was open to a man who seemed old enough to be his father.

"Life coach? What exactly is that line of work, Frank?" Jason asked.

"Not so much a line of work but a way of life. Life coaching is what I was designed to do. Now, coffee—that is where my experience makes me an income. My good friend owns a coffee-buying company, and I fly to where the beans are grown. I guess the good Lord has given me the ability to recognize and savor a fine cup of joe. I also enjoy the buying end of the industry. But helping others as a life coach is my passion and my purpose."

The very concept of having a passion and purpose irritated and convicted Jason all at the same time. He thought he had passion when he started his company, but his only purpose was to be successful. Now he wondered what success really was.

"I've learned a lot about your business, Jason. But tell me, how is life?"

Jason thought, "What a question, and what do I say?" So he gave his usual default answer. "Life is good; I can't complain."

After such a genuine exchange the answer seemed cheap, even to Jason. It definitely got the attention of Frank, who looked into Jason's eyes and said, "I would guess that someone as detail-oriented and driven as you, Jason, would have a lot to say about life."

Jason knew Frank had his number and was relieved when Frank said, "If there's ever a time you could use some encouragement, I'd be happy to help."

Frank's offer was warm and refreshing. "Actually I'm a little confused about direction," Jason said, "especially after talking with you. There is a hurdle I need to get over. But I'll get through it; it's no biggie."

The overhead speaker interrupted their brief silence. "We are approaching LAX and will land in fifteen minutes."

As Jason stowed his laptop, Frank turned to him and said, "Do you mind if I pray for you, Jason?"

Before Jason could think it over, he heard himself say, "Sure, no problem."

As Frank prayed, Jason actually *felt* something. He was unsure of what it was, but he knew Frank's prayer was unlike anything he had ever heard. The prayers he remembered from his childhood were lifeless and repetitive. He mouthed the words as his mom recited those "Now I lay me down to sleep" types of prayers. But this was different. Frank spoke like someone with an inside connection to God. He prayed very specific things over Jason, things Jason had not mentioned to him. It was weird yet powerful and very encouraging.

After they landed, Jason's cell phone fired off notifications for the many text messages, emails, and voice messages that awaited his reconnection to the network. As he climbed into a cab, he scrolled through the notifications to see what needed his immediate attention. He listened to all of Cindy's voicemails, not once but twice. He truly missed her, and now she was just forty-five minutes away!

For some unknown reason Jason skipped his usual stop to pick up a six-pack. Talking with Frank Benson had affected his thinking somehow. The thought of drinking or doing anything that seemed controversial was out of the question.

"What if Frank calls and asks what I'm doing?" Jason wondered as he neared the house. Excited as he was to see Cindy, his encounter with Frank still occupied his mind.

Help Wanted

The lie (or deception) of independence is based on self-help philosophies. Self-helpers believe they can get themselves through anything with the right motivation and inspiration. Of course God gave us powerful minds and the free will to make choices. Yet when left to our own devices, our self-accountability is too easily manipulated by our shifting moods and feelings.

Recently I saw video footage from a massive train wreck played all over the news. One thing was certain: those train cars could not get themselves back on track. An engineer with an independent spirit would cause only greater harm and ensure the train would remain stuck forever. He or she would have to admit the train was broken and needed outside help.

As much as the devil would have liked to kill Jason outright, he knew that physically killing him was not necessary. He needed only to derail Jason's forward movement. One of the most effective methods was to use Jason's own pride to feed his spirit of independence. If the devil could keep Jason from seeking and accepting help, he could keep Jason off track indefinitely (more on this in chapter 13).

Proverbs 16:18 could not be any clearer: "Pride goes before destruction, and a haughty spirit before stumbling." Life's disappointments, especially the disappointing acts of others, help us to become distrustful and self-reliant. If we distrust others, we will inevitably distrust God. Coupled with our pride, this distrust fuels an independent spirit.

Pride is a stronghold that partners with independence. Like twin brothers working in perfect synergy, pride and independence convince us we can never be derailed (that happens only to other people). Even when the unthinkable happens, pride and independence convince us we can get back on track all by ourselves.

Such is the independent posture so prevalent in the current culture, both in and out of the church. The famous last words that haunt many self-empowered, independent Christians are "No help wanted. I've got this!"

CHAPTER 10
HERITAGE THEFT

You are my hiding place; You preserve me from trouble;
You surround me with songs of deliverance. Selah.
—PSALM 32:7

MORE THAN TWO months had passed since Jason met Frank Benson on the flight home from Asia. Although Jason's conviction about drinking lasted only a couple of days, the conversation with Frank kept rolling around in his mind, especially the prayer Frank prayed over him.

Jason could have used that prayer many times since that day. This seemed like one of those times.

"Are you OK?" he asked his wife.

Jason sensed Cindy was bothered by something. Maybe he noticed it because he'd begun spending more time at home.

"I'm fine," she answered.

Jason admitted having little or no understanding of the female language, but he was sure of one thing: "I'm fine" never means "I'm fine."

Jason tried again. "What's up, baby? You seem a little off your game."

With worry and frustration in her voice Cindy answered,

"I'm pregnant. But like we discussed, I'll take care of the problem."

Cindy's words revealed some inner controversy over what she adamantly claimed to believe. Growing up in California public schools, she'd been indoctrinated early on to believe the thing growing inside her was not a baby but some unwanted tissue. So why was she suddenly tense over it?

It had taken awhile for Jason to come around to Cindy's way of thinking, but they had finally agreed to delay starting a family until it was convenient for both of them. What Jason did not know was that back in college Cindy had an inconvenient pregnancy. To the delight of her mother and then boyfriend she promptly took care of the problem. To this day she had never mentioned it to Jason or her father.

Now the memory and secrecy of that choice were messing with her head. Especially during the past week she'd tried to tamp down her emotions around Jason, but to say she was in turmoil would be an understatement.

Cindy had used contraceptives throughout her married life. Yet she was pregnant. This was what she and Jason had pre-labeled as an accident—the kind of pregnancy they would "correct" if it ever happened to them.

When and if they ever had kids, it would be on their terms and in their timing.

Scientific and Biblical Reality

Aborting a blessing is probably not what any woman seeking an abortion wants. However, until you understand each life is fearfully and wonderfully made by God, it is hard to recognize pregnancy as the blessing it is.

For Christians, purposefully destroying what God has created is not an option. So the enemy cloaks the truth by labeling God's beautiful creation as a blob of flesh, something not technically alive yet. These pressures are compounded by a media environment that feeds a culture of carnality and is nourished by it.

The stunning reality is that even the moral commitment of many in the body of Christ has been tainted despite the true facts of life. Let's take a look at some of those facts, as they relate to human conception and development in the womb:

Day 1: Fertilization: all human chromosomes present; unique human life begins.

Day 6: Embryo begins implantation in the uterus.

Day 22: Heart begins to beat with the child's own blood, often a different blood type than the mother's....

Week 5: Eyes, legs, and hands begin to develop....

Week 8: Every organ is in place, bones begin to replace cartilage, and fingerprints begin to form....

Weeks 9 and 10: Teeth begin to form, fingernails develop. The baby can turn his head, and frown....

Weeks 10 and 11: The baby can "breathe" amniotic fluid and urinate. Week 11 the baby can grasp objects placed in its hand....

Week 17: The baby can have dream (REM) sleep.[1]

Even though these facts are medically proven, a segment of the population (even within the church) propagates the idea that such tissue in the mother's womb is not a human life. Interestingly some of the same people who swear by these ideas also fight for day-old bald eagle eggs to be protected the same way full-grown eagles are.

Just try removing an egg from an eagle's nest and see how quickly our government rescues the defenseless, unborn bird. The public's outrage over such cruelty is matched by a staggering maximum fine of $250,000 and two years in prison for felony violations of the Bald and Golden Eagle Protection Act.[2]

These kinds of stories become national headlines (not a strategy I would recommend for garnering publicity). And, for the record, you can get busted for possessing a bald eagle eggshell or a feather you might find on the ground,[3] but ripping a baby from the womb is acceptable. As wonderful as these birds are, should an eggshell or feather be better protected than an unborn human being?

Let me clarify my personal point of view. I have had countless encounters with these magnificent birds. With the world's largest population of bald eagles living in Alaska (an estimated thirty thousand according to the Alaska Department of Fish and Game[4]), I find it difficult to avoid these majestic wonders. I have literally spent weeks studying their habits in the wilderness of this state. My personal favorite is the golden eagle. I have gained a healthy respect and love for these high flyers after watching them close up and not merely reading about them in a magazine article. With that being said, I still believe human life is of greater value.

If you disagree with my last statement, please don't toss the book out the window just yet. Take a moment to look with me at the spiritual view of the creation process, which civil societies honored without question for millennia.

In Jeremiah 1:4–5 the prophet Jeremiah says, "The word

of the LORD came to me, saying, 'Before I formed you in the womb I knew you, and before you were born I consecrated you; I have appointed you a prophet to the nations.'"

This truth is a template for all humankind. The Creator's methods of putting us together have not changed. He has repeated the process billions of times. Even so, each of us is different and has a unique purpose in life. The key is that all of us are made in His image (Gen. 1:26), and as Jeremiah 1:5 shows, Father God knew us even before we were conceived!

The word translated "knew" in Jeremiah 1:5 is the Greek word *yada`*, meaning "to know...to know by experience...to know, be acquainted with."[5] I was in my thirties when I received a deep revelation of this passage. I recall asking God (not really expecting an answer), "God, what were You doing in there?"

I was simply thinking out loud and was not ready for His quick response. "I was planting seeds of destiny!" He seemed to speak so clearly to me. I remember scrambling for a pen or pencil to capture His words, which brought much biblical understanding and also spiritual alignment to many areas of my life.

If that verse is not convincing enough, consider this amazing passage:

> You created my inmost being; you knit me together in my mother's womb. I praise you because I am fearfully and wonderfully made; your works are wonderful, I know that full well.
>
> —PSALM 139:13–14, NIV

God was and is all-knowing. He knows every baby personally and intimately. Yes, He was personally acquainted with you even before He formed you by His hands in your mother's womb! Those divine seeds of destiny are planted deep within your DNA by a loving heavenly Father. When we allow heaven's truth and God's love to water them, a metamorphosis occurs in our lives.

The truth is that Cindy never had anyone she could talk to about her abortion experience, so she learned to hide her emotional meltdowns over the years. They say time heals. Well, Cindy was convinced that whoever "they" were, they were wrong. Every time the anniversary of her abortion came along, Cindy would privately quake under the weight of the memories and emotions.

When those anniversaries and seemingly random situations triggered old memories, she wondered, "Why does it still hurt? If it's OK to end a pregnancy, why is so much guilt attached, and why won't it go away?"

When she first discovered she was pregnant back in college, the issue seemed so uncomplicated: make the call, schedule the appointment, and in one short visit her little problem would be gone.

Yet it had not worked out that way. Now years later she wanted desperately to share her feelings with Jason but was unsure of what he might think of her hidden past. "Maybe I can talk to Joyce," she muttered as she cleaned up another botched attempt at dinner. "Maybe this week."

Thursdays had become her time with Joyce, and Cindy always looked forward to it. Now as their lunch date approached, she hoped to muster the courage to expose this painful part of her past to her friend. "If I can't trust Joyce, then I can't trust anyone," she thought.

Just then the phone rang. "Hey, Joyce!" Cindy answered.

"I'm sorry to call so late, Cindy, but I was hoping that we

could move our lunch date to Wednesday. Keith leaves on an emergency mission trip this Thursday and I want to see him off. Would Wednesday work for you?"

Cindy was relieved Joyce didn't cancel altogether, and getting together a day early was perfect. "That would be great, Joyce! Same place and time?"

———◆———

At best the decision to take a life for the sake of personal convenience is sad. When that decision is made hundreds of thousands of times each year, much more is at issue than a political agenda or a woman's right to choose. The enemy's foundational purpose for abortion has always been to slaughter a generation, which perfectly serves his mission to steal, kill, and destroy. It is personal to Satan; he will continue to exterminate God's children before they understand their God-given authority to bring his hellish works to a screeching halt.

As long as we allow it, he will continue to decimate our families and godly lineage. He will ruthlessly rob generation after generation of its rightful heritage.

The Healing of Forgiveness

Halfway through their special Wednesday lunch, Joyce asked, "Is everything OK, Cindy?"

"Sure. It's all good."

Cindy could tell Joyce was not convinced. She knew her body language sometimes gave her away, and Joyce always seemed to know when something was eating at her. So she just admitted it. "Actually there is something I need to share with you, but it's not coming out so easily."

Over the next hour she took Joyce through the entire

backstory of her abortion. When she was done, she asked plaintively, "Now what?"

Joyce held one of Cindy's hands as Cindy opened her heart. The emotions had caught Cindy off guard. Yet she felt the weight lifting as she disclosed her past. As she felt it go, she realized for the first time just how much internal pressure she had endured for all those years.

"Has this really affected me so deeply?" she wondered as she experienced new relief.

The compassion Cindy felt from Joyce made the disclosure much easier than she had expected. Although she recognized fresh feelings of deep loss, an inexplicable comfort seemed to soak her soul.

"'Now what?' is a great question to ask, Cindy. Before we talk about that, I want to tell you how very proud I am of you! This was a brave move. You might not know it yet, but you have taken your first step toward emotional healing."

As Joyce spoke, Cindy felt her emotions shift from deep concern to even greater relief.

"Now for your question," Joyce continued. "The answer might not be as easy as it sounds, but it is absolutely necessary for the healing of your heart to begin. Are you ready?"

Cindy responded with an eager "Yes!"

"Well, you've already done step one: you told your story. Step two is to forgive everyone involved—your old boyfriend, your mother, and anyone who pressured you to make this choice."

Step two registered with Cindy, but Joyce apparently wanted to make sure. "Are you tracking with me?"

"Yes. I'm with you."

"OK, because step three is the toughest one of all." Joyce paused for what seemed like forever. "Step three is all about forgiving yourself."

Cindy's shoulders sank slightly.

"When you forgive yourself," Joyce continued, "you will enter a whole new dimension of hope for the future. Mastering this step will position you for success in step four."

Like a sponge Cindy absorbed every word Joyce said. The steps made perfect sense, and her heart seemed to confirm them. "You're right, Joyce. Forgiving myself is the hardest part. I had no idea that I was harboring unforgiveness toward myself all these years! It explains why the guilt never really left me."

As Cindy clenched her coffee cup with both hands, she could sense the power of this revelation collapsing the walls of pain that had enclosed her heart.

After a few minutes of silence Cindy smiled and asked, "OK, so what is step four?"

With her smile beaming from across the table, Joyce responded. "Step four is the follow-through that most Christians won't commit to. The forgiveness steps are about your inner healing, but unless you make step four the foundation of your life, unforgiveness could regain its power over you."

"Tell me already!" Cindy cried out expectantly.

Cindy's outburst made both women dissolve into laughter. When Joyce recovered, she said, "OK, girl. OK! Here it is: Move forward in life, and let Jesus take the reins from here on out. He not only wants to heal the wounds of the past; He wants to bless your future! So let Him bless you!"

"You're right, Joyce. That sounds too easy."

"Exactly. The reward is not in the hearing but the *doing*. Most believers won't allow Jesus to *really* take the controls. In one way or another they keep a firm grip on the steering wheel. Then they wonder why they keep ending up in the ditch that runs beside their destiny road."

Cindy identified with what Joyce was saying.

"You see, it's really about trust—trusting that Father God has no axe to grind because of your past and trusting Him to guide you from now on. You can't trust Him that way unless you believe He truly loves you and wants the best for you. That's the heart of a true Father. He doesn't love you because you do everything right; He loves you because you're His daughter!"

The revelation of love overwhelmed Cindy. She beamed with joy as Joyce formed each word. A high tide of freedom arose inside her like nothing she had ever known.

The feeling was interrupted momentarily by the fact that she still had more to share. "Joyce, this has been so wonderful! I'm so blessed by your words, and I so appreciate the way you make things totally clear and easy to understand."

"Do I sense a 'but' coming?"

"There is one more thing I need to tell you."

———————•———————

Cindy understood the need to forgive her ex-boyfriend, but forgiving herself was another matter. She could not see that happening. The hardest person (for her and for us) to forgive is the one in the mirror.

The guilt Cindy felt was not generated by her family, her friends, or even a church. The home and church environments in which she was raised took no issue with abortion and never disparaged anyone for making that choice. So if her politically correct indoctrination did not cause her sense of shame and guilt, what did?

Could it be that Cindy's Creator had been speaking heavenly truths to her inner heart all those years? Was God's Holy Spirit confirming the difference between right and wrong in her spirit? Had the inner struggle been evidence of her past choices battling against the divine truths embedded in her very being?

I believe the answer is yes. That is why the four steps Joyce described resonated with Cindy and released her from her pain. Biblical principles ring true when our hearts are open. To the degree we embrace God's love and His pure laws, we experience emotional healing and the freedom to enter a blessed future.

The hardest person to forgive is the one in the mirror.

So remember these four steps and use them often:

Step one: tell your story.

Step two: forgive others.

Step three: forgive yourself.

Step four: trust Father God with your future.

Step four is beautifully mapped out in a Scripture passage definitely worth repeating: "Trust in the LORD with all your heart and do not lean on your own understanding. In all your ways acknowledge Him, and He will make your paths straight" (Prov. 3:5–6).

Is that not a mouthful? Let's look more closely at the components of step four:

- *Trust in the Lord.* This is how we move forward. It means trusting the fact that God is for us and not against us.

- *...with all your heart.* This speaks to the level at which we should trust the Lord. *All* of our

133

hearts means *all*! Putting some of our trust in Him and the rest in our jobs, the economy, other people, or ourselves never ever works the way we would like it to.

- *Do not lean on your own understanding.* This eliminates any option to believe that our life experiences or self-generated wisdom can yield the best results. The statement demands that we step away from any politically correct indoctrination and humanistic mind-sets we have embraced over the years.

- *In all your ways acknowledge Him.* This means keeping our eyes on where God is leading us, not where we have been.

- *He will make your paths straight.* Obedience to the previous portions of the passage ensures that He will straighten our paths. In a world of confusing twists and forks in the road Father God Himself will give us a straight path with clarity in our life purpose.

———•———

Cindy's meeting with Joyce gave her a lot to process and pray about, so she took the long way home. Disclosing her pregnancy was so much easier than she imagined it would be. Joyce's refusal to lecture her made all the difference. Really all she said was, "Seek the voice of the Lord, Cindy, and ask Him for His peace to accompany the right choice."

Cindy felt clear-eyed and empowered. "I know what to do," she said softly while parked at a favorite vista point. She had come to this place before to get away and think. However, this time was different from all the rest. This time she sensed the strong peace of God surrounding the decision she knew was right. It was the very peace Joyce had talked about, a peace stronger than any accompanying any other decision she'd ever made.

"Lord, help me to tell Jason. Help me, Jesus. I'm scared!"

This was Cindy's prayer as she headed home. This talk with Jason would be the most serious one they'd ever had and would test the very fabric of their marriage.

———————◆———————

Please understand that the enemy despises you. He hates the family unit exemplified in the pages of Scripture. Satan is effectively using abortion to destroy the God-designed family! It is heritage theft, and it is part of his ultimate plan. He knows the fight to save one baby at a time starts with healing one woman at a time from the inner pain of abortion.

No wonder he works so hard to deceive, control, and conquer women like Cindy!

CHAPTER 11

THE JESUS ADDENDUM

If you are not disciplined—and everyone under-
goes discipline—then you are not legiti-
mate, not true sons and daughters at all.
—HEBREWS 12:8, NIV

THIS TRIP WAS a first for Cindy and Jason, and she was excited about it. Her renewed relationship with her father was growing stronger, and she convinced Jason to join her and her dad for a weekend at the coast. Jason had no issues with his father-in-law; he'd simply had no access to him. Cindy had written off her dad long before she married, and until recently she avoided all conversation about him.

The three-hour drive to the shore would also give Cindy time to talk out the pregnancy matter more fully. Since her meeting with Joyce, she had come clean about her past. To her surprise Jason responded with a kind of love and concern she had never seen from him. Now she hoped he was still open to discussing it.

With some trepidation she broached the subject. "Honey, I know you wanted to pray about this before our trip. Are you ready to talk about it?"

Without missing a beat, Jason laid out his thought process. Cindy did not always understand Jason's way of thinking, but she had learned to appreciate it over the years.

"Yes, I prayed about it, like on every run after work, every commute, and most of last night. I was a little ticked at first that you kept it from me. But then I thought about how you held the pain inside all that time. It made how I was feeling seem a little lame."

Jason had Cindy's complete attention as he continued.

"I know we had planned to control the timing of a family, and we agreed ahead of time that if an abortion was necessary, then we would do that. But that was then and this is now. What I'm trying to say is... Well, you know that 'peace of God' thing the pastor's wife talks about? Well, I really think I'm noticing that peace, especially when I think of us having a baby."

Cindy tried to hide her tears, but overwhelming feelings of joy, relief, and peace got the best of her.

Jason quickly pulled over. "Baby, are you OK?"

Wanting to know what kind of tears she was crying, he took her hand and asked, "Are these good tears?"

With large drops running down her puffy face, Cindy smiled and said, "We are going to have this baby!"

Their joy and excitement built as they talked through all the details for the rest of their road trip. When they got to the subject of baby names, a ring interrupted them, courtesy of Bluetooth.

"Hello, Frank," Jason answered cheerfully.

It was Frank Benson.

"You've been on my heart the past few days, Jason. I thought I'd give you a call."

Jason had mentioned Frank Benson to Cindy, but this was

the first time she heard his voice. She knew God had used this man, whom she had never met, to minister to her husband. For that she was grateful.

She waited for a gap in their conversation and then jumped in. "Hi, Frank! This is Cindy. So good to finally meet you—well, on the phone anyway."

Frank was so kind and told her several endearing stories Jason had shared about her. The man had a way about him that they both loved. As if trying to keep the conversation from ending, Jason and Cindy seemed to tag team him with questions. They enjoyed the comforting sound of his voice and loved how his answers were filled with wisdom.

The conversation went from one subject to another. At one point Jason asked him, "How do I avoid compromise in my business? There's so much pressure to comply with clients' demands."

Frank didn't miss a beat. "I would imagine that the pressure to bend your lifestyle toward political correctness is continual. The only answer is found in your love, Jason. When you find yourself in love with Father God, then your heart will be concerned with scriptural correctness and sickened by cultural demands."

Frank had the perspective of someone who'd been around awhile. "You kids live in a generation that accepts carnality, worldliness, compromise, and addictions and then accepts Jesus as a kind of additive that makes everything OK."

"Wow. That is spot on," Cindy responded softly.

What Frank said convicted them both and brought such clarity!

Scripturally Correct vs. Politically Correct

An unhealthy tolerance for politically correct sin has crept into the Western church. Pleasing people rather than God is becoming more prevalent, even within the walls of the Christian community. This fear-driven stance motivates Christians to acquiesce to an ever-evolving moral gauge.

There may be several factors playing into the Western church's compliance with the world. However, I propose that I am accurate in saying it is foundationally fear driven. Fear is what keeps us from aligning with the truth of the Bible and standing tall for what we believe is scripturally correct. That same fear—the fear of man—keeps us conformed to the common directional flow of our culture.

In chapter 12 of the Book of John we see that although Jesus performed many signs, people did not profess belief in Him. Verse 42 says, "Nevertheless many even of the rulers believed in Him, but because of the Pharisees they were not confessing Him, for fear that they would be put out of the synagogue."

Are you getting this? The very spiritual leaders who believed in Jesus kept their mouths shut because they feared retribution and the loss of their positions. It makes sense because the fear of man is fueled by the need for approval. Approval is not inherently bad. It is one of the ways God shows His own approval. When we crave approval, however—no matter how hidden the desire might be—it ultimately controls our moral compass.

If leaders in the early church struggled with this weakness, it should not surprise us that church leaders struggle with it today. The real question is, Why would a Christian fear man?

The answer is in John 12:43: "for they loved the approval of men *rather* than the approval of God" (emphasis added). Ouch! That statement just might leave a mark! Whether or not we know it, we were designed by Father God to desire approval—*His* approval. When we need or desire more than that, we venture into dangerous realms of man-pleasing.

> I am amazed that you are so quickly deserting Him who called you by the grace of Christ, for a different gospel; which is really not another; only there are some who are disturbing you and want to distort the gospel of Christ. But even if we, or an angel from heaven, should preach to you a gospel contrary to what we have preached to you, he is to be accursed! As we have said before, so I say again now, if any man is preaching to you a gospel contrary to what you received, he is to be accursed! For am I now seeking the favor of men, or of God? Or am I striving to please men? If I were still trying to please men, I would not be a bond-servant of Christ.
> —GALATIANS 1:6–10

I appreciate that the apostle Paul admitted his former attempts to please people. The pressure on him as a spiritual leader to placate his colleagues was as prevalent then as it is now. Becoming a bondservant of Christ meant not being a slave of religion and tradition.

Complying with a culture compromises your ability to transform it.

While his former fear of man showed in his attempt to please men, his new love for his Savior caused him to please God, no matter who disapproved.

The fear of the Lord is not prevalent when the fear of man is in operation. Simply put, the fear of man will cause you to comply with anything that qualifies you for earthly approval and makes you feel safe from rejection. But beware. Complying with a culture compromises your ability to transform it.

———————◆———————

Jason and Cindy were riveted to their conversation with Frank on the way to the coast. Never missing a beat, Frank continued, "Jesus has no desire to be an added ingredient in our lifestyles. He went to the cross to model a sacrificial life and bring us total transformation. He did not do all that to become an afterthought or addendum. His work on the cross was the ultimate revelation of His love for humankind."

"The man is making total sense!" Jason thought.

"As our love for Him grows, our hatred for all that hurts Him grows too. When we live on the edge, testing how close we can get to sin without being burned, it shows that our love for our heavenly Father is also on the margins. We live on the edge of sinning when our love for the world is uppermost in our hearts. I loved my wife with a passion, and to the same degree I hated the sickness that hurt her. When you really love someone, you hate whatever threatens their well-being. Therefore sin hurts the very heart of God. As our love for Him grows, so does our hate for all that hurts Him."

Frank certainly had a way of explaining things.

"So you see, Jason, that it's all about love."

"Wow," Jason responded. "For me that means taking a stand and going against the corporate flow!"

Frank went silent long enough for Jason and Cindy to wonder whether they'd lost the connection. Then he picked up right where he left off. "Living separate or apart from the world has always been the goal, kids. The trend of modifying Scripture to align with culture is infecting the purity and power of the Christian life. The Christian example can be revived to its intended value only by us."

Frank was earnest. "You see, folks, when people like us

commit to living apart from the world's standard and raising up a standard of love for Jesus, then we will transform our surroundings. That Christlike lifestyle postures us not to dilute Scripture so it aligns with the culture but to modify culture until it aligns with Scripture. Living the love of God through Jesus is what changes lives!"

Walking the Talk

Non-Christians seem to know what Christians should and should not do. They understand Christians should not have the same habits, interests, music, entertainment, language, and lifestyle as they do. If they can't find any differences between their lifestyles and ours, then what is the draw? What would attract them to our way of life? If they see in believers a reflection of themselves, then the word *Christian* is just another title.

Frank Benson is right: Jesus has no desire to be an addendum to our lifestyles. Adding Jesus to our mix of preferences was never part of His plan.

An addendum is a kind of supplement. The dictionary says it is "a thing to be added; an addition; an appendix to a book."[1] Jesus is not a thing to be added or tacked on to something else. If adding Jesus to our mess had been the Father's plan, then the very costly work of the cross was nothing more than a squishy gospel of self-change that offers no real freedom from the enemy's grip. It would be (and is for some) a Christianity that never beckons us to follow a *holy* Savior.

I'm not implying holiness is or should be our main pursuit. On the contrary we should pursue the very heart of God! When we move toward a lifestyle of loving what He loves and hating what He hates, then holiness is the inevitable by-product.

I remember a youth pastor whose outward appearance

143

showed what he believed: that he had to mirror those he was trying to influence. When the pants of the Western teen culture hung lower, so did his. If a colorful Mohawk or a spiked mullet was the fad, he had one. Unfortunately his copycat methodology was limiting to his ministry, not because of his style choices but because you can't lead what you are following.

The drive to meet Cindy's father went much faster than expected. Jason and Cindy's phone time with Frank felt like a spiritual and emotional feast. Combined with their decision to bring their baby to term, they could barely contain themselves.

You can't lead what you are following.

"I'm going to be a dad!" Jason blurted out while Cindy confirmed reservations at her dad's favorite little villa overlooking the sea.

Cindy's smile was larger and more beautiful than ever as she listened to Jason go on about fatherhood. When they arrived at their destination, Cindy's dad stood near the entrance, waiting to greet them. The smile on his face made it obvious he was looking forward to their time together.

Charles opened the passenger door and gave his daughter a big daddy hug. "How's my little pumpkin?"

Cindy glowed and was so pleased to be with her father again. The weather was perfect for lunch on the deck, and it was a great place to talk with him. Charles reached across the table and held his daughter's hands as she told him the entire backstory of her abortion.

"Pumpkin, I'm so sorry you went through that alone. I wish your mother would have told me."

Forgiveness was requested and given on both ends several times during the course of the conversation. Jason remained mostly silent during the father-daughter exchanges but was pleased at his father-in-law's responses, especially when tears gave way to laughter with news of Cindy's current pregnancy.

"I'm ready to negotiate for grandfather time!" Charles said gleefully.

"Dad, you can have all the time you want," Jason piped up. "We just need to get ready for this whole baby thing."

As they walked the beach after lunch, Cindy interrupted the new baby conversation and asked her dad, "Why do you think Mother pushed for the abortion and then kept it from you, Daddy?"

He stopped in his tracks and turned to Cindy, "I don't fully understand it, pumpkin. Maybe she was afraid of what I might say or what others might think. When I met your mother, her religious beliefs would have kept her from encouraging an abortion. I think people change. They even put their beliefs on the back burner when it suits them. I confess I have often ignored the voice that keeps telling me to do the right thing. And I've been thinking about that more often lately."

Simply Push the Button

So many Christians use what I call "the button" that turns their Christianity on and off. Though their forefathers in the faith lived the Word of God as a lifestyle, many followers of Christ today follow Him only when it's socially appropriate or culturally correct. When they "do church" each week, they simply turn on the spiritual juice for about ninety minutes.

I am truly amazed at how quickly and how often the button is pressed on and off. I recall an evening service filled with youth and young adults aggressively going after the presence of God in worship. It was an anointed service, but within minutes afterward many of those young people gathered in a darkened room to invest equal passion in a movie filled with witchcraft, sorcery, demonic beings, nudity, and filthy language. Apparently they saw the church service as God's time and the after-service hours as their time.

When I confronted them about this, several in the group passionately defended the movie and justified the content. Obviously they had pushed the button and successfully switched on their other love.

Pushing that button sometimes results from other people's influence. A teenage boy in our youth ministry heard a clear directive from the Lord to remove the TV from his room. He came to me and shared how the Lord convicted him of his addiction to demonic and sexual content he watched late at night. He had been deeply affected by the powerful move of God in our youth service and was excited to get home and remove this stumbling block. I explained he could not unilaterally dispose of property that was not his. He explained he bought the TV with his own money and it was in his room. The set was his.

When he attempted to remove it, however, his mother (a Christian) told him he was overreacting and was moved only by emotion. "Just give it some time, and see if you still feel the same way in a few days," she told her son.

Moved by emotion? Of course he was! When God speaks, you should be moved by emotion. The shortest scripture in the Bible shows that Jesus was moved by emotion. It says, "Jesus wept" (John 11:35).

The young high schooler listened to his mom and put off the urgency he sensed from the Holy Spirit to remove demonic inroads in his life. Ultimately he fell deeper into his visual addictions and continued to struggle with pornography through his adulthood.

The truth is that his mother was fearful. If she had accepted her son's convictions, it would have challenged her own compromises. That was just not going to happen. Spiritually insecure parents are often intimidated when their children raise the banner of holiness higher than they do.

When the power of conviction comes on us, it is for our benefit—to free us, heal us, and empower us! If we desire the fullness of all that God has for us, prompt obedience to His voice is necessary. Our quick responses to His guidance can be lifesavers, *literally*. (We will explore more on hearing the voice of God in chapter 12.)

When the Holy Spirit speaks to us, we do not have the luxury of responding when we feel like it. Jesus wants to free us from our prisons. During those times of anointing, our cell doors are flung wide open so we can escape the bondage that holds us. Delaying our exit because we might be overreacting and emotional is not what people behind bars think about.

There will always be professing Christians—maybe well-meaning moms or even pastors—who are intimidated when other people's convictions exceed their own. People like that will go out of their way to keep your standards and mine lower than theirs.

I remember a time when we encouraged holiness and admired believers who raised the bar. We celebrated people who reached for greater levels of obedience, and we appreciated when they challenged us to strive for standards worthy of our high calling. Now Christians who pursue holy living are considered unrealistic and radical and are even mocked for such ideas—not by unbelievers but by Christians.

To accept the idea (the biblical command) of pursuing a sinless life means falling out of love with this world. With regret I propose that most people who carry the "Christian Club Card" find that idea to be outrageous, impractical, and weird. Such is the condition of the larger Western church and an American Christian culture steered by cultural trendsetters. Both are too willing to accept compromise.

You probably know your share of button pushers. If so, you can see the meaning of Christian has been diluted over the past few decades and is now up for grabs. This is happening in a generation that plucks scriptures from the Bible that make them feel comfortable in their lifestyle and their sin. This is largely due to the abandonment of absolutes from generation to generation. The trend is inherently dangerous because the Word of God is full of absolutes that provide us with transparent definitions of *right* and *wrong*.

A glaring example in our culture is the academic equalization movement that makes sure every student gets an A, every kid is a winner, and nobody loses. This is actually a smoke screen for eliminating personal accountability and relieving people of its demands. Unfortunately, rewarding students' lack of work with unearned As is teaching them the basic lessons of selfishness and entitlement.

This type of indoctrination claims that one person's intentions are of equal value to another person's performance. With that mind-set individuals decide what is right and what is wrong. Their Creator no longer defines such standards; instead they believe standards are subjective. Of course subjective standards are inherently unreliable, which leads the culture toward confusion and fabricated controversy.

This is happening in our world right now, and we are already tasting its bitter fruit.

CHAPTER 12
PAST THE NOISE

Your ears will hear a word behind you, "This is the way, walk in it," whenever you turn to the right or to the left.
—Isaiah 30:21

THE WEEKEND WITH Cindy's father had been good for all three of them. Now several months later Jason was deep in the process of reprioritizing his life and having weekly talks with Frank, which continued to produce much emotional and spiritual breakthrough.

At first Jason did not realize he needed either kind. Now, however, he'd made some significant changes. He sold many of his overseas accounts and hired an overseas sales manager, moves that allowed him more time at home.

Cindy had also changed. More interested in their future as a family, she was also more engaged in homemaking than ever before and even practiced making new dishes for Jason. The motivation came easily with his working locally and coming home for dinner each night.

Tonight's dinner was extra special—it was Friday night and they were celebrating Jason's birthday.

"Dinner was perfect, baby. That roasted duck was *amazing!*"

Jason grew up duck hunting. He shared his fondness of home-cooked duck on several occasions, so Cindy went all out to surprise him. The dinner was a great success, and now the two of them cuddled on the sofa and enjoyed some after-dinner coffee.

It may have been slow in coming, but there was a healthy change in their home. After one of his talks with Frank, Jason accepted a challenge: he removed alcohol from his home and from his business encounters. He also filtered his entertainment choices more carefully and steadily pruned his movie collection.

We have a natural tendency to follow the voice with which we are most familiar.

"I'm so proud of you, sweetie!" Cindy said gratefully. "You have made some big sacrifices."

Jason gazed downward at his coffee and replied, "Thanks, babe. For the first time in my life I think I have been hearing God. Not like out loud but more like a clear voice in my head. Maybe He was always there speaking and I'm just now realizing it."

Looking up with a gentle smile, he added, "I think we're heading in the right direction."

Recognizing God's Voice

We have a natural tendency to follow the voice with which we are most familiar. I would propose that the very purpose of the written Word of God is to take us back to Eden—not the geographical location but a relational state in which the Father's voice *is* familiar. God wants His kids to learn His voice and communicate openly with Him.

> This day I call the heavens and the earth as witnesses
> against you that I have set before you life and death,
> blessings and curses. Now choose life, so that you and
> your children may live and that you may love the LORD
> your God, *listen to his voice*, and hold fast to him. For the
> LORD is your life, and he will give you many years in the
> land he swore to give to your fathers, Abraham, Isaac
> and Jacob.
> —DEUTERONOMY 30:19–20, NIV, EMPHASIS ADDED

Do you see how listening to the Lord's voice is our very life? Father God never desired a cold, distant relationship with us. For the record, He never designed a system that limited His children to hearing Him through others, be it in Latin or any other language. Yet unless you learn to hear God's voice, you will be forever dependent on the voices of others!

> Then Moses cried out to the LORD, and the LORD showed
> him a piece of wood. He threw it into the water, and
> the water became fit to drink. There the LORD issued
> a ruling and instruction for them and put them to the
> test. He said, *"If you listen carefully to the LORD your God
> and do what is right in his eyes, if you pay attention to his
> commands and keep all his decrees*, I will not bring on you
> any of the diseases I brought on the Egyptians, for I am
> the LORD, who heals you."
> —EXODUS 15:25–26, NIV, EMPHASIS ADDED

Hey, but that's Old Testament! Yes it is, and through the Old and New Testaments we find a heavenly Father who wants to connect personally with His sons and daughters. Jesus was our perfect example; He continually followed the voice and direction of His Father.

Learning to hear the voice of God is easier than most

people would expect. Think about it: if Father God desires to converse with us, why would He make discerning His voice difficult? Of course we should schedule times of being still and listening for His voice, but as we become more familiar with its sound, we will easily distinguish it from life's noise.

Let me tell you a story.

It was 11 p.m. on a cold, dark night in late September 1999. For two days I had ridden my dual sport motorcycle for hundreds of miles on challenging roads in and around Denali National Park, a huge expanse of Alaskan wilderness. Battling adverse conditions on my trek north had taken its toll, and I wanted to find a safe place in the woods to camp for the night.

Recognizing my own exhaustion, I kept my speed at forty-five miles per hour and scanned the shoulders of the lonely highway both for wildlife and a safe place to pull into the woods. Glad to be out of Denali's sixty-mile-per-hour winds, I was now focused on getting some sleep. There was no traffic; the only sounds I heard were from the cold wind blowing through my helmet, the low rumble of my four-cycle engine, and the slapping of my bike's off-road knobby tires on the pavement.

Then loud and clear out of nowhere I heard a voice say, "Slow down!"

Though I was physically and mentally worn, I knew enough to respond to the voice that sliced through the sounds in my helmet. So I shifted into a lower gear.

About a minute later the same voice spoke the same two words: "Slow down!"

I shifted down another gear. Now traveling at about thirty miles per hour, I heard the voice again. "Slow down!" I grabbed a still lower gear.

Creeping along at twenty miles per hour, I saw my little

headlight reflecting off a steel bridge ahead. As I approached the entrance of the bridge, I heard the clear request again. This time it was a little louder and more intense. "Slow down!"

By this time I knew I was either hearing the Lord's voice or had officially lost my mind.

In first gear and moving at about ten miles per hour, I drove onto the bridge only to find it completely blocked by a massive grizzly bear at the other end! Because of my slower speed I was able to grab the clutch with my left hand and make a safe stop about ten yards from the very large, ominous predator. (Although I sat high in the saddle of my off-road motorcycle and the grizzly was planted on all fours, he stood taller than I.)

Keeping both lanes blocked, the bear stared into my flickering headlight for about three minutes. It felt like hours. I had no reverse option, and darting either left or right would have sent me into the forbidding currents of the river. The .357 Magnum I'd tucked under layers of off-road winter gear felt more like a peashooter than a deadly weapon because if that grizzly moved toward me, I could not possibly draw it in time. Thirty feet is nothing to an animal capable of accelerating to thirty-five miles per hour from a dead stop!

When the bear decided I was not worth his effort, he very slowly moved off the road and into the trees. Shortly after his rear end disappeared into the woods, I made my move and broke my zero-to-sixty speed record. For the next twenty miles I held the throttle to the bike's maximum speed and finally made camp for the night.

As I lay under the stars in my sleeping bag, I knew the Lord had spared my life. He had a hope for me, plans and a future meant not to bring harm but life! And if I allowed Him to direct my path, He would use me for the benefit of many others. It was just as the prophet Jeremiah said in quoting

Him: "'For I know the plans I have for you,' declares the LORD, 'plans to prosper you and not to harm you, plans to give you hope and a future'" (Jer. 29:11, NIV).

God's voice is our life source *if we recognize it*. His desire from the beginning was to speak with us. The purpose of His written Word is to reveal His person and establish us in relationship with Him—to take us back to the garden experience where we can walk and talk with our Creator, as it was in the beginning.

Father God has been speaking to His kids ever since! As we grow closer to Him, we recognize His voice more and more, just as sheep learn to recognize their shepherd. Scripture says that "when he has brought his own sheep outside, he walks on before them, and the sheep follow him *because they know his voice*" (John 10:4, AMPC, emphasis added).

We always follow the voice we have trained our inner (spiritual) ear to hear. This training determines whom we believe and whom we don't.

> You do not believe because you are not of My sheep. My sheep hear My voice, and I know them, and they follow Me; and I give eternal life to them, and they will never perish; and no one will snatch them out of My hand.
> —JOHN 10:26–28

Whether you have been a Christian for years or are still discovering who Jesus is, the point Jesus was making in John 10 is that those who know Him follow Him. And to follow Him, we must learn His voice.

The enemy wants to take you and me out of the picture because he's threatened by our heavenly callings and purpose-filled destinies! The enemy knows that if he can keep us from hearing God's voice, we will never act on what God says.

———————◆———————

Cindy secured their favorite window table, and Joyce arrived right on schedule as usual.

"I already ordered your coffee," Cindy mentioned as they hugged.

From Cindy's perspective these hugs had started as social courtesies, but now they represented sincere love and gratitude. Cindy's heart was open to Joyce, who always asked questions with authenticity. Cindy had grown to appreciate this and their friendship immensely, and she looked forward to every meeting.

"You were right, Joyce," Cindy said as they settled into conversation. "I think praying over my marriage and family is really making a difference."

Looking pleased to hear it, Joyce used both hands to hold her cup close to her mouth. Cindy had learned this was Joyce's listening mode, so she continued.

"Jason and I have been talking a lot lately about hearing God's voice, and we both feel like we are getting better at it. But how do you really know when it's God who's directing you? It's hard to decipher sometimes."

Joyce set down her cup and responded. "That's a great question. How I wish more people would ask it! But you're right. With all the busyness of life and the many voices yelling into our ears, it can be hard to pick the right one to follow."

Cindy waited for the detail she knew was coming.

"Here is what Keith and I do. We use a tool to confirm the voice of God, and it has worked really well. We call it the measuring stick."

Cindy jumped in as Joyce took a sip. "The measuring stick?"

Joyce lowered her cup and continued with a smile. "The measuring stick we use is one word—*peace!*"

Cindy sat back as if Joyce's answer was a bit too simple.

"Cindy, think about it. Would a loving heavenly Father give His children peace about doing something He doesn't want them to do? Heavenly peace comes from Father God. You could say it accompanies the direction in which He desires us to go. As the Bible says, this peace goes beyond our understanding. It can calm our spirits right in the middle of a storm."

God's Voice Comes With His Peace

Joyce paraphrased Philippians 4:7, which says, "The peace of God, which surpasses all comprehension, will guard your hearts and your minds in Christ Jesus." Apparently, if peace guards our hearts and minds, a lack of peace leaves our hearts and minds unprotected against the onslaught of the enemy.

This peace Joyce described can be a true indicator we have singled out God's voice from the sea of voices swirling around us. No matter how many voices there are, there will always be a dominant voice that influences us the most. As the sheep of His pasture the dominant voice for us should be the Shepherd's.

> The gatekeeper opens the gate for him, and the sheep listen to his voice. He calls his own sheep by name and leads them out. When he has brought out all his own, he goes on ahead of them, and his sheep follow him because they know his voice. But they will never follow a stranger; in fact, they will run away from him because they do not recognize a stranger's voice.
>
> —JOHN 10:3–5, NIV

I was a teenager in the mid-1970s and worked part-time at a private ranch with twelve horses that were about as dysfunctional a herd as you could imagine. The ranch was owned by a local church my father pastored, and it was my job to feed this motley crew at 7:00 a.m. and 5:00 p.m. every single day.

The horses were part of a program that served kids on Saturdays. People donated horses that had issues they no longer wanted to deal with. So they gladly blessed the ranch with the beasts. The dominant horse was an Appaloosa named Old Blue. He ruled the ranch, and like his underlings he responded to no one except me.

When people called the horses from the fence, it didn't matter how loud they whistled or how many apples they offered; they could cajole those animals in every possible way but to no avail. Old Blue and his gang responded only to the voice they knew best, which was mine. When they were out of sight and grazing on the back forty, all I had to do was whistle and they would come running. They could distinguish my scent, my whistle, and my voice from anyone else's.

In other words the horses had a relationship with me that was deeper than what they shared with other people who visited the ranch. They spent more time with me and were fed by me. They trusted me. I remember a morning when the fog was so thick, I had trouble finding the barn and placing the feed hay. There was no way to see the horses or for them to see me. Yet I had to whistle only once, and all twelve ran to me.

They trusted my voice so much that they were willing to run blind in the fog. They knew that if they responded, they would be safe and well fed.

This is the desire of Father God: for us be so familiar with the Holy Spirit's voice that we hear it past the noise and the fog of life. Even when we cannot see the path—through times of confusion, seasons of darkness, and attacks of the enemy—the voice of our loving Creator will guide us.

You might be in the middle of a fog right now with a blanket of confusion obscuring your situation. Yet in this very moment the Holy Spirit is speaking comfort, healing, and direction.

Hearing, recognizing, and obeying God's voice brings protection, provision, and promotion.

You might not be able to see what's ahead, but you can trust His voice to lead you in the right direction. Your relationship with Him makes all the difference, as Jesus explained:

I know My own and My own know Me, even as the Father knows Me and I know the Father; and I lay down My life for the sheep. I have other sheep, which are not of this fold; I must bring them also, and they will hear My voice; and they will become one flock with one shepherd. For this reason the Father loves Me, because I lay down My life so that I may take it again.

—JOHN 10:14–17

Knowing God always outweighs our needs. It is about more than our personal needs, however. It is about the many people who have yet to join His heavenly flock. As you and I recognize and obey His voice, many others will find the same peace, and we will experience protection, provision, and promotion like never before. Yes! Hearing, recognizing, and obeying God's voice brings protection, provision, and promotion.

As a Father, He is *that* good!

CHAPTER 13

A NEW BREED

A person's wisdom yields patience; it is to
one's glory to overlook an offense.
—PROVERBS 19:11, NIV

URING THE WEEK following Jason's birthday, Cindy kept reminding him she had planned something special for Saturday. As their coffee time ended on Friday morning, she mentioned it again.

Jason knew she was up to something but had no clue what it might be. "Just what are you planning behind my back, babe?"

Cindy responded with a knowing smile. "A very special surprise for my birthday boy. You'll just have to wait to find out what it is."

Saturday came quickly. When the phone rang at the stroke of noon, Cindy knew it had to be her mom.

After some small talk Mom returned to her new favorite subject. "I can't believe you told your father before you told me! You should have told me first! I'm going to be a grandmother, and I find out from my ex?"

The subject had become Gina's theme song, and Cindy had had her fill. "We've already covered this, Mother! I don't need to explain myself again and again."

Gina would not let up.

"Really, Mom, it's time for you to move on and remember that your ex just happens to be my father!"

Gina was deeply offended by the "ordeal" of not being the first to know about the baby. She was equally unhappy about Cindy's renewed relationship with her father. "You have really hurt my feelings, and on top of all of that you haven't gone shopping with me on Saturday in...well, forever!"

The wounded victim theme was nothing new. It was the lifelong platform from which Gina launched all of her manipulation and control. Cindy knew the drill. So she turned on her phone's speaker function, set the phone on the counter, and continued prepping for Jason's surprise dinner.

Gina proceeded to spew a litany of offenses and her usual rhetoric about each of them. Not soon enough Jason entered the kitchen and gave Cindy the karate-swipe-across-the-throat signal to end the call, knowing the conversation was nothing but an irritation to his wife.

Only too happy to oblige, Cindy started the difficult process of ending the call by telling her mother, "I'm so sorry you are hurt and offended, but there is nothing more I can do for you, Mother! Maybe you should pray about how you feel."

Gina did not even acknowledge the suggestion.

"I've got to go now. I love you, Mother. Talk to you later. Bye."

Jason was impressed by how Cindy took control and ended the call. "It's not your fault, baby. Your mom has been offended as long as I've known her."

The Offense Fence

All of her life Cindy spent precious energy trying not to upset or offend her mother. Her efforts were fruitless of course. No matter what you do, wounded people will be easily offended and will choose to stay that way.

Today we live in the most offended culture ever! Offense sways politics, inspires our laws, and destroys relationships. Offended unbelievers should not surprise us, but when those who call themselves Christians walk in continual offense, we know we have a grave problem.

The gospel offends the proud and defends the humble.

For the record, Jesus had every right to be offended. And if anyone had the right to carry His offenses through His whole life, He did! His own people went out of their way to offend Him *on purpose*! They spit on Him, mocked Him, and gambled for His clothing. They hung Him on a cross to suffer the most painful death ever because of *our* sin. Then, when He was parched from thirst, they gave Him vinegar instead of water.

That would be reason enough for me to carry an offense forever. Yet after all of that and in the middle of His undeserved torment, Jesus said, "Father, forgive them; for they do not know what they are doing" (Luke 23:34).

His response is *stunning*!

You see, Jesus knew what we must always remember: that the gospel offends the proud and defends the humble. The people who participated in Jesus' execution were offended by the gospel, but God's truth defended and exalted Him.

That does not mean we should share the gospel just to offend people. It simply means that if you speak the truth (especially the truth of God's Word), some people will be offended! Being intimidated by that possibility should never keep us from moving in obedience to the Lord's voice, however.

Many church leaders have stifled the vision of local churches (and the church at large) simply because they fear offending people. The story is not new. In Jesus' day the Pharisees and other religious leaders were offended often.

> Then some Pharisees and teachers of the law came to Jesus from Jerusalem and asked, "Why do your disciples break the tradition of the elders? They don't wash their hands before they eat!"
>
> Jesus replied, "And why do you break the command of God for the sake of your tradition? For God said, 'Honor your father and mother' and 'Anyone who curses their father or mother is to be put to death.' But you say that if anyone declares that what might have been used to help their father or mother is 'devoted to God,' they are not to 'honor their father or mother' with it. Thus you nullify the word of God for the sake of your tradition. You hypocrites! Isaiah was right when he prophesied about you: 'These people honor me with their lips, but their hearts are far from me. They worship me in vain; their teachings are merely human rules.'"
>
> Jesus called the crowd to him and said, "Listen and understand. What goes into someone's mouth does not defile them, but what comes out of their mouth, that is what defiles them."
>
> Then the disciples came to him and asked, "Do you know that the Pharisees were offended when they heard this?"
>
> He replied, "Every plant that my heavenly Father has not planted will be pulled up by the roots. Leave them; they are blind guides. If the blind lead the blind, both will fall into a pit."
>
> —MATTHEW 15:1–14, NIV

This was not the answer Jesus' detractors expected. His lack of political correctness appalled them. Yet Jesus never said, "Oh no! I'm sorry I offended you. I didn't mean to hurt your feelings. I take back what I said. Please accept My apologies."

If our Lord apologized every time He offended someone, He never would have fulfilled His heavenly purpose or obeyed the Father. The same is true if He labored under every offense that was hurled at Him. Remember: Jesus had every right to be offended; He simply chose not to be. At times you have every right to be offended too. Yet the strongest Christians are the hardest to offend.

Several conditions can position us not only to be offended but also to live under the weight of offense. Let's look at a few of them:

Fear

Some common fears are fear of the future, fear of the past, fear of failure, and fear of people (and what they might think). Fearful people have a negative bent and like to play the devil's advocate. Their fear feeds their paranoia, and it ensures their continued state of offense.

Religion

Jesus' fiercest opposition came from the religious community in His culture. Merely following religious tradition for the sake of doing what has always been done keeps one living in the past, whereas the relationship Jesus offers frees people into their futures.

Anger is a common action or reaction of the religious that rarely manifests itself in the presence of joy. Nehemiah 8:10 says, "Do not be grieved, for the joy of the LORD is your strength." If the joy of the Lord is our strength, then many believers are weak, and many are angry and openly drawing offense.

Self-focus

The selfishness of an inward focus works against the Christian life. Jesus exemplified the selfless life we are to choose. Those operating in selfishness are easily offended. When vision and concern are limited to one's view in the mirror, life becomes dark and shallow.

The self-focused desire is not to serve but to be served. Jesus showed us a lifestyle of true servanthood, which is contrary to the self-focused posture that operates in victimization. The self-focused person assigns accountability to others but never to self.

Insecurity

Insecurity produces a thin skin—a fragile emotional veneer that is easily bruised by others and forces them to walk on eggshells. The common ploy of the insecure is manipulation, which is used for self-protection. However, it does not work indefinitely. As already mentioned, the enemy breaches your security through your insecurity.

Jealousy

Jealous means "feeling of resentment against someone because of that person's rivalry, success, or advantages."[1] Jealousy puts a chip on one's shoulder and keeps it there. It searches for reasons to be offended by the advancement, blessings, or favor others receive. This is in contrast to the biblical command to "be devoted to one another in brotherly love; give preference to one another in honor" (Rom. 12:10).

Criticalness

Offended people lean toward being critical. The views and ways of the critic come easily for them. Believers who are offense magnets display their insecurities through their jealousies and criticisms of others.

Unforgiveness

Unforgiveness fuels stress, which infects any social environment. Because of their unresolved hurts many Christians live daily with unforgiving hearts. They do not realize forgiveness is more beneficial to the offended party than the offender. Jesus didn't wait until everyone asked His forgiveness for nailing Him to the cross; He freely offered it! It's not about other people deserving forgiveness. Just as Jesus forgave us, we should forgive those who have offended us.

You may have heard it said that not forgiving others is like drinking rat poison and then waiting for the rat to die. Forgiving others is not an option for the Christian; actually it is a command and a salvation issue. You see, unless Father God forgives us, we are doomed. And remember what Jesus said: "If you do not forgive others, then your Father will not forgive your transgressions" (Matt. 6:15).

Far too many Christians are trapped in the pit of unforgiveness, in part because of the "soft gospel" being served to them. They may not be aware that withholding forgiveness is a sin. Yes, I said it. To live in unforgiveness is to live in sin. We must check ourselves and always remember that forgiveness is a lifestyle, not an event!

I propose that when Jesus forgave humankind on the cross, it was not His first round of forgiveness. He had lived a life of forgiveness, and it was part of His methodology. He understood forgiveness preserves us. When offense is left to grow and fester, it develops an impenetrable wall that aggressively rejects love, compassion, and (need I mention?) accountability. Many church leaders struggle with hurt and sometimes unknowingly live in offense because they are withholding their forgiveness. People might be impressed by these leaders' gifts and skills in the pulpit, for example, but these abilities will eventually be smothered under the blanket of negativity fueled by offense. Offense builds a fence around your heart.

———————◆———————

Jason looked for things to do around the kitchen—anything that might uncover clues about the coming surprise.

"You sure are overly helpful today, honey," Cindy noted.

Jason took his search to the back patio. "Hey! What's with the third place setting?" He thought, "Finally a real clue!"

Offense builds a fence around your heart.

"You'll find out soon, honey. Would you please pour the iced tea?"

Jason had run out of reasons to snoop around, and Cindy was not about to cave to his barrage of questions.

"I'll get it!" Jason blurted when the doorbell rang.

Cindy removed her apron, followed him to the door, and pulled out her smartphone to capture the moment.

Of all the possibilities Jason had pondered, he never imagined this one. "No way! I can't believe you're here! You're actually *here*!" Jason kept repeating himself as he embraced Frank.

"Welcome to our home, Mr. Benson," Cindy said with a loving voice and hug.

"It's Frank to you, young lady. Let's not be too formal."

Jason was still processing his excitement as they made their way to the patio. He had not seen Frank since they met on that flight from Asia.

"Baby, you really got me. It's so great to have you here, Frank!"

Over dinner they caught up on everything. Jason and Cindy even roped Frank into the baby-name discussion. Then Frank unintentionally turned the conversation in a heavy direction.

"How are your parents, Cindy?"

Cindy started off with great reports about her relationship with her father and how much healing there had been in a short few months. Cindy knew Frank was asking about her mom too; there was no way around it.

After an awkward pause she said, "Mother is Mother. I can't seem to make her happy. I love her, but her constant manipulation is wearing on me. She is so easily offended at everything and everyone. I guess I'm just tired of navigating around her emotions."

Frank listened as Cindy asked the inevitable question: "What do you think, Frank? Am I overreacting?"

Frank smiled and turned to Jason. "Is that coffee ready? I think this answer might take awhile."

For a moment Jason seemed mostly concerned with how Frank would rate his coffee-brewing skills. "You're the coffee expert, Frank, so go easy on me, OK?"

Jason's nervous smile eased when Frank flashed a big grin and a thumbs up. "You did a great job, young man. We just might have a place for you in the company! Now let me attempt to answer your question, Cindy. First of all, your feelings and reaction to your mother are normal. No one enjoys manipulation. And offended people share certain habits. For one they strive to receive attention, honor, and even position. They believe that anyone who seems to enjoy peace, happiness, or blessing somehow received what should have been theirs."

That made sense to Cindy.

"Your mother doesn't realize that the very thing she wants can come only after the very thing she needs, which is repentance. You see, repentance leads to healing, and healing leads to promotion."

Cindy hung on every word.

"Your mother, like so many people, needs healing from the past. Those past hurts, whether they are real or perceived to be real, give offense a landing place in her heart."

Frank quickly looked up a verse on his smartphone. "Here it is. Proverbs 26:2: 'Like a sparrow in its flitting, like a swallow in its flying, so a curse without cause does not alight.' In other words a curse or offense needs something to land on—a former scar, a hurt, or a past pain. In most cases these unresolved issues breed unforgiveness."

Jason and Cindy absorbed every detail of what Frank said.

"Have you ever stubbed your toe?" he asked.

They nodded.

"We bump our toes on furniture, steps, you name it. People even step on our toes! But we go on with life because the pain is not great enough to demand our attention. When the toe is actually injured—it might be bruised or swollen or sensitive to touch—we finally give it the attention it needs to heal. Emotional wounds are just as real as an injured toe, and until they are healed, even the slightest bump or perceived infraction causes throbbing pain."

After requesting a second cup of coffee, Frank explained, "One of the challenges when dealing with offended people is to keep yourself from becoming offended by them."

Cindy instantly identified with Frank's words. "I really needed to hear that, Frank. I can feel the offense creeping up inside me whenever my mother goes off on one of her rants. Why does she get under my skin so easily?"

Frank replied, "That's an easy one: those closest to you have the most power and potential to offend you."

The Unoffendables

When the Sabbath came, he began to teach in the synagogue, and many who heard him were amazed. "Where
did this man get these things?" they asked. "What's
this wisdom that has been given him? What are these
remarkable miracles he is performing? Isn't this the carpenter? Isn't this Mary's son and the brother of James,
Joseph, Judas and Simon? Aren't his sisters here with
us?" And they took *offense* at him.

Jesus said to them, "A prophet is not without honor
except in his own town, among his relatives and in his
own home."

—MARK 6:2–4, NIV, EMPHASIS ADDED

Christians should not be surprised when family members
are easily offended. As was true for Cindy's mother, familiarity can breed a lack of faith and devalue the people we
know best. But imagine for a moment the complete opposite:
Christians who cannot be offended by what others say. How
great would that be, and is it even possible?

Well, isn't that the lifestyle Jesus exemplified for us? Didn't
He expect us to follow His lead? Of course! So let's imagine
this new breed of unoffendable Christians in some detail! It is
really quite simple. They are believers who:

- trust their hearts in the hands of Jesus

- keep their eyes on their divine purpose

- are not distracted by the emotional tricks of the
  enemy

- do not create drama or get caught up in other
  people's drama

169

- follow Jesus and quickly forgive the offenses of others

To be unoffendable, you have to recognize offenses and resist them. So what does the dictionary say about the word *offense*? Here is a partial definition: "a violation or breaking of a social or moral rule; transgression; sin; a transgression of the law; misdemeanor; a cause of transgression or wrong; something that offends or displeases."[2]

Offenses will always come our way. It is never a matter of *if* but of *how often*. Until we forgive, offense leads us to dishonor others, which is to offend them in return. Dishonoring those whom you feel have offended you is the easiest and most common response you can choose. When you take on an offense, a motive of revenge brews within you and becomes a root of bitterness. This bitter root invites the demonic to speak lies to your soul. When those lies are empowered by belief, they take control of your heart.

This has happened to far too many Christians; they have cultivated the bitter root of unforgiveness, and it has suffocated unity. In addition to eroding unity, offense actively empowers division. These dual actions eat away at the foundations of our faith and attack the soundness of the body of Christ.

Division within Christian circles is not only painful, but it also keeps us compromising our faith, which in turn prevents us from becoming the strong army of God! When the Pharisees tried to link Jesus to the demonic, Jesus knew exactly what they were thinking. He said to them, "Every kingdom divided against itself will be ruined, and every city or household divided against itself will not stand" (Matt. 12:25, NIV).

Let me propose an idea that sounds outrageous and seems

unobtainable but that Jesus successfully accomplished: let's become superheroes!

No, I haven't lost my mind. I am talking about becoming a new breed of Christians who are completely unoffendable! Our superhero name is obvious: the Unoffendables.

OK, I may have lost some of you on this one, but hang in there and think about it. Because of what Jesus did on the cross, we have already lost our right and privilege to be offended. If the enemy needs only to keep us offended in order to hold us down, then we need to fight back like the superheroes we are called to be!

I'm not talking about wearing capes, neon tights, or T-shirts emblazoned with the letter *U*. The Bible has already laid out our superhero gear—it is the armor of God.

> Finally, be strong in the Lord and in the strength of His might. Put on the full armor of God, so that you will be able to stand firm against the schemes of the devil. For our struggle is not against flesh and blood, but against the rulers, against the powers, against the world forces of this darkness, against the spiritual forces of wickedness in the heavenly places. Therefore, take up the full armor of God, so that you will be able to resist in the evil day, and having done everything, to stand firm. Stand firm therefore, having girded your loins with truth, and having put on the breastplate of righteousness, and having shod your feet with the preparation of the gospel of peace; in addition to all, taking up the shield of faith with which you will be able to extinguish all the flaming arrows of the evil one. And take the helmet of salvation, and the sword of the Spirit, which is the word of God.
>
> With all prayer and petition pray at all times in the Spirit, and with this in view, be on the alert with all

perseverance and petition for all the saints, and pray on my behalf, that utterance may be given to me in the opening of my mouth, to make known with boldness the mystery of the gospel, for which I am an ambassador in chains; that in proclaiming it I may speak boldly, as I ought to speak.

—EPHESIANS 6:10–20

What does an Unoffendable look like? Exactly like you or me, the modern Christian decked out in the armor of God.

———————•———————

After dinner the men joined Cindy in the kitchen to clean up.

"So was our surprise a success, sweetie?" Cindy asked Jason, even though she knew the answer.

"Affirmative, baby! I still can't believe Frank is actually here."

Jason and Cindy beamed as they and Frank finished tidying up, but the discussion of offense was not over yet.

"Your insight has been so helpful, Frank, but exactly how do you know when you have forgiven someone?" Cindy's question was heartfelt. "And how do I live out this forgiveness? It's really tough to do when people...well, when my mother brings up the same issues over and over again."

They headed to the living room, comforted in the belief that Frank had an answer. He had become more than a friend or spiritual coach; he was like a father to Jason and Cindy.

"I think you're asking two different questions, Cindy, so let me tackle the first one. You know you have forgiven when you have the memory of the pain without the pain of the memory."

Frank let that settle in for a moment and then rephrased it. "Let's try it this way. You know you have forgiven someone when you have the memory of the pain that once hurt but no longer feel the pain of that memory."

Jason and Cindy got it, and Frank kept going.

"Let's talk trains for a minute." With that Frank accepted a slice of his favorite pie.

Cindy had done her homework and learned pecan pie was his favorite dessert.

"This must be homemade!" Frank said as he savored his first bite.

"Yes," said Cindy. "It's homemade, but I had some help from a neighbor."

Jason chuckled and Frank continued. "Yum. Now where was I? Oh yes, I was about to talk trains, and who doesn't like trains?"

Jason and Cindy wondered where Frank was going with the train thing.

"I think this example will answer your second question, Cindy. Years ago when

You know you have forgiven when you have the memory of the pain without the pain of the memory.

I was traveling in Alaska, I met a retired train engineer who tried his best to answer my many questions, as I have a fondness for trains. We talked about the different seasons and the challenges they bring to railroaders. I asked him how they got through the snowdrifts that are so common in mountain areas. What he shared made a real impact on me."

Jason put down his pie and stared intently at Frank. Cindy giggled because she knew what Jason was thinking. It was the same thing she was thinking: "Get to the story, Frank!"

"You see, trains are massive and weigh hundreds of tons. Yet a train is no match for a large snowdrift on the tracks. A snowdrift can build up under the locomotive and lift it off the track, derailing the train. Once a train's derailed, it can't get back on track by itself! Some very specialized heavy equipment has to be called in."

Knowing his audience was intrigued, Frank continued. "This equipment is very hard to schedule, and the logistics of getting it to the accident site can be astronomical. The retired engineer told me about a derailment in the Northeast. It took more than six months and plenty of equipment for crews to clean up that wreckage! The point my engineer friend was driving home is this: derailed trains cannot help themselves."

Jason enjoyed another bite of pie and piped in. "So how do they run trains in the winter? Do they shut them down when it snows?"

"That's what I was wondering. Because trains don't have much defense against snowdrifts, they are fitted with snowplows. And here's what really fascinates me: the design of the snowplow causes the weight of the snowdrift to put downward pressure on the front of the train, which helps it to stay on the track. The very thing that once threatened to derail the train now helps keep it safe. Isn't that amazing?"

Jason gave Cindy that clueless look, and she returned it.

"I'm sure you've heard the phrase *got off track*. Well, let me share with you the lesson, or revelation if you will, that the Lord spoke to me after I learned about the train's snowplow. Imagine you are the train, the train track is your destiny road, and snowdrifts are the offenses of life. Life and the people in it cause offenses to pile up on our destiny road. We know from the train example that these snowdrifts threaten our forward movement. We also know that although our enemy, the devil, would like to physically kill us, he knows that he doesn't have to. He can stop us just by getting us off track!"

Frank took another bite of pie and gave his audience the "Are you with me?" look.

Jason and Cindy nodded, their eyes wide open.

"If the enemy can use offense to keep us walking in hurt and withholding forgiveness, he can derail us. He knows that derailment kills our forward movement. It keeps us in emergency mode and keeps us from our God-given mandate! That old engineer revealed that when the train, which is us, is fitted with a snowplow, the piles of offense, hurt, pain, unfair treatment, neglect, and abuse that were designed to derail us are neutralized. The plow pushes aside the very thing that challenged our purpose! It lifts the snow—the offense—and directs it away from the tracks. It clears the path to our destiny."

Frank looked at them and ate the remaining crust of his pecan pie. "God has a purpose for you. The enemy wants to stop any forward advancement on your destiny road. So here is the lesson to live by: we are the train; offense is the snowdrift; and the snowplow is our forgiveness!"

———•———

When we become Unoffendables, other people's actions can no longer derail us. That is great because being derailed is no fun. To *derail* means "to cause (a train, streetcar, etc.) to run off the rails of a track; to cause to fail or become deflected from a purpose; reduce or delay the chances for success or development of...to become derailed; go astray."[3]

Maybe you need to get on track toward your destiny again. Maybe you feel like an upended train: your life is wrecked and your wheels are spinning, but you are going nowhere. Are you tired of it? Then take heart! Jesus is here to heal your heart of every offense and restore your direction. He stands ready with His specialized heavy equipment. His love, grace, and forgiveness will get you back on track.

If you have been derailed or gone astray, this is your divine moment. If the Holy Spirit has spoken to your heart through this book, now is the time to make Jesus not just an addendum but the Lord of your life.

The track of your destiny road is unique and designed just for you. It is filled with amazing adventures, healing, and purpose. Yes! Your life really matters. Is it time for *you* to join this new breed of Jesus followers? I can't see why not.

The next step is up to you.

CONCLUSION
THE NEXT STEP

UNDERSTANDING OUR PLACE in Christ has confused too many people for too long. In his book *He Qualifies You!* Chad Mansbridge simplifies our misunderstanding of our connection to a holy God through three covenants that describe our connection to Him:

- Under the Abrahamic Covenant; God's promises become your right and inheritance, because of your *pedigree*.

- Under the Mosaic Law Covenant; God's promises are your right and inheritance, because of your *performance*.

- But under the New Covenant Agreement, through the Gospel of Jesus; God's promised blessings are your right and inheritance, purely because of your *position* [in Christ].[1]

In the third covenant your access to the Father is not about the church you attend or the sect that defines you. Your relationship with Father God is defined solely by your position in and through His Son, Jesus Christ.

> Not everyone who says to Me, "Lord, Lord," will enter
> the kingdom of heaven, but he who does the will of My
> Father who is in heaven will enter. Many will say to Me
> on that day, "Lord, Lord, did we not prophesy in Your
> name, and in Your name cast out demons, and in Your
> name perform many miracles?" And then I will declare
> to them, "I never knew you; depart from Me, you who
> practice lawlessness."
>
> —MATTHEW 7:21–23

Our position with our loving heavenly Father is not found
through our experiences or defined by our family beliefs. Our
history cannot bring us into right relationship with God, nor
can our culture point us in the right direction. Instead we
must make a commitment to a new position in Christ, as the
apostle Paul explains:

> If you confess with your mouth Jesus as Lord, and
> believe in your heart that God raised Him from the dead,
> you will be saved; for with the heart a person believes,
> resulting in righteousness, and with the mouth he con-
> fesses, resulting in salvation. For the Scripture says,
> "Whoever believes in Him will not be disappointed." For
> there is no distinction between Jew and Greek; for the
> same Lord is Lord of all, abounding in riches for all who
> call on Him; for "Whoever will call on the name of the
> Lord will be saved."
>
> —ROMANS 10:9–13

I invite you to position yourself *in Jesus* today! Today is the
day of salvation, and God's Holy Spirit is calling you into the
arms of a forgiving and loving heavenly Father. Whether you
need to get back on track or step onto your destiny road for
the first time, today is your day!

———————◆———————

If you responded to this invitation by asking Jesus to be the Lord of your life, please email me at RonPrattAlaska@gmail .com. I'd like to personally congratulate you! You can also reach me at www.RonPrattAlaska.com.

NOTES

Chapter 1: The Christian Family

1. Joseph S. Exell, *The Biblical Illustrator: The Minor Prophets* (Grand Rapids, MI: Baker Book House, 1960), Hosea 7, https://www.studylight.org/commentaries/tbi/hosea-7. html.
2. Dictionary.com, s.v. "critical," accessed November 5, 2018, https://www.dictionary.com/browse/critical?s=t.

Chapter 2: The Media Trap

1. Evan Beck, "10 Infectious Diseases That Changed History," Listverse, January 19, 2018, http://listverse. com/2018/01/19/10-infectious-diseases-that-changed-history/.
2. Rebecca L. Collins et al., "Does Watching Sex on Television Influence Teens' Sexual Activity?," RAND Corporation, 2004, https://www.rand.org/pubs/research_briefs/RB9068.html.
3. Rani Molla, "Next Year, People Will Spend More Time Online Than They Will Watching TV. That's a First," Recode, June 8, 2018, https://www.recode. net/2018/6/8/17441288/internet-time-spent-tv-zenith-data-media.

Chapter 3: A Newfound Freedom

1. David Wilkerson, *Sipping Saints: A Challenge to Drinking Christians* (Lindale, TX: Wilkerson Trust Publications, 1978), 11.
2. Dictionary.com, s.v. "encumbrance," accessed November 8, 2018, https://www.dictionary.com/browse /encumbrance.
3. Kenny Luck, "Beer, Bubbly and Libation Lies—But God's Not a Buzzkill," Every Man Ministries, March 31, 2014, https://www.everymanministries.com/blog/emm-main-blog/beer-bubbly-and-libation-liesbut-gods-not-a -buzzkill.

4. Vladimir Poznyak and Dag Revke, eds., "Global Status Report on Alcohol and Health 2018," World Health Organization, 2018, http://apps.who.int/iris/bitstream/handle/10665/274603/9789241565639-eng.pdf?ua=1.

5. Nina Larson, "Alcohol Kills One Person Every 10 Seconds Worldwide: World Health Organisation," *Sydney Morning Herald*, May 13, 2014, https://www.smh.com.au/lifestyle/health-and-wellness/alcohol-kills-one-person-every-10-seconds-worldwide-world-health-organisation-20140513-zrapl.html.

6. Poznyak and Revke, "Global Status Report on Alcohol and Health 2018," xv.

7. Dictionary.com, s.v. "legalism," accessed November 9, 2018, https://www.dictionary.com/browse/legalism?s=t.

8. Dictionary.com, s.v. "religion," accessed November 9, 2018, https://www.dictionary.com/browse/religion?s=t.

Chapter 4: Growing Cold

1. *California Driver Handbook* (Sacramento, CA: Department of Motor Vehicles, 2018), 99, https://www.dmv.ca.gov/web/eng_pdf/dl600.pdf.

2. "DUI & DWI," DMV.org, accessed November 9, 2018, https://www.dmv.org/automotive-law/dui.php.

3. *California Driver Handbook*, 99. Chart reprinted with permission from the California Department of Motor Vehicles.

4. "BAC Chart: Actions Resulting in Loss of License Alcohol Impairment Charts Driving Under the Influence of Alcohol and/or Drugs /Is Illegal," University of California Regents, accessed October 22, 2018, https://studentwellness.uci.edu/wp-content/uploads/2015/04/BAC-Chart.pdf.

5. Dictionary.com, s.v. "moderation," accessed November 9, 2018, https://www.dictionary.com/browse/moderation?s=t.

6. Dictionary.com, s.v. "moderator," accessed November 9, 2018, https://www.dictionary.com/browse/moderator?s=t.

7. Dictionary.com, s.v. "moderate," accessed November 9, 2018, https://www.dictionary.com/browse/moderate?s=t.

8. Alaska Statutes 2017, AS 28.35.280, http://www.akleg. gov/basis/statutes.asp#28.35.261.

9. *The Truth About Alcohol* (Los Angeles: Foundation for a Drug-Free World, 2015), 19, https://www.drugfreeworld. org/FURL/data/www.drugfreeworld.org/files/truth-about-alcohol-booklet-en.pdf.

10. Poznyak and Revke, "Global Status Report on Alcohol and Health 2018," 221.

11. National Center for Statistics and Analysis, *Alcohol-Impaired Driving: 2016 Data*, Traffic Safety Facts no. DOT HS 812 450, National Highway Traffic Safety Administration, October 2017, https://crashstats.nhtsa.dot.gov/ Api/Public/ViewPublication/812450.

12. Blue Letter Bible, s.v. *"pisteuō,"* accessed November 9, 2018, https://www.blueletterbible.org/lang/lexicon /lexicon.cfm?Strongs=G4100&t=KJV.

13. Blue Letter Bible, s.v. *"skandalizō,"* accessed November 9, 2018, https://www.blueletterbible.org/lang/lexicon /lexicon.cfm?Strongs=G4624&t=KJV.

Chapter 5: Hollywood or Holy Word?

1. Dictionary.com, s.v. "carnal," accessed November 10, 2018, https://www.dictionary.com/browse/carnal.

2. Your Dictionary, s.v. "carnal," accessed November 10, 2018, http://www.yourdictionary.com/carnal.

3. Blue Letter Bible, s.v. *"parakaleō,"* November 10, 2018, https://www.blueletterbible.org/lang/lexicon/lexicon. cfm?Strongs=G3870&t=KJV.

4. Blue Letter Bible, s.v. *"anakainōsis,"* accessed November 10, 2018, https://www.blueletterbible.org/lang/lexicon/ lexicon.cfm?Strongs=G342&t=KJV.

5. Matt Blitz, "A Brief History of the Movie Rating System," Today I Found Out, December 30, 2014, https:// gizmodo.com/a-brief-history-of-the-movie-rating-system-1676334900.

6. Blitz, "A Brief History of the Movie Rating System."

7. Blitz, "A Brief History of the Movie Rating System"; Linda Alchin, "Hays Code," Siteseen Limited, updated January 9, 2018, http://www.american-historama. org/1929-1945-depression-ww2-era/hays-code.htm.

8. Blitz, "A Brief History of the Movie Rating System."

9. "History of Ratings," MPAA, accessed November 10, 2018, https://filmratings.com/History.

10. Blitz, "A Brief History of the Movie Rating System."

11. "Film Ratings," Motion Picture Association of America, Inc., accessed November 10, 2018, https://www.mpaa. org/film-ratings/.

12. "Classification and Rating Rules," Motion Picture Association of America, Inc. and National Association of Theatre Owners, Inc., revised January 1, 2010, https://www. filmratings.com/Content/Downloads/rating_rules.pdf.

13. "What Do Movie Ratings Mean, and Who Applies Them?," HowStuffWorks, accessed November 10, 2018, https:// entertainment.howstuffworks.com/question467.htm; "Classification and Rating Rules," Motion Picture Association of America, Inc. and National Association of Theatre Owners, Inc.

14. "Classification and Rating Rules," Motion Picture Association of America, Inc. and National Association of Theatre Owners, Inc.

15. Dick Rolfe, "Hollywood Uplink—November 2007: The Ratings History of 'NC-17 vs. 'X,'" Dove Foundation, November 2007, https://dove.org/hollywood-uplink-november-2007-the-ratings-history-of-nc-17-vs-x/.

16. Rolfe, "Hollywood Uplink—November 2007."

17. Rolfe, "Hollywood Uplink—November 2007."

18. "Harry Potter and the Deathly Hallows: Part 1—Parents Guide," IMDb, accessed November 10, 2018, https:// www.imdb.com/title/tt0926084/parentalguide.

Chapter 6: Seduced by Deception

1. Dictionary.com, s.v. "compliment," accessed November 10, 2018, https://www.dictionary.com/browse/ compliment?s=t.

2. Dictionary.com, s.v. "flirtation," accessed November 10, 2018, https://www.dictionary.com/browse/flirtation?s=t.

3. Dictionary.com, s.v. "coquetry," accessed November 10, 2018, https://www.dictionary.com/browse/coquetry.

4. *Collins English Dictionary*, s.v. "flirt," accessed November 10, 2018, https://www.collinsdictionary.com/us /dictionary/english/flirt.

5. Dictionary.com, s.v. "seduce," accessed November 10, 2018, https://www.dictionary.com/browse/seduce.

6. *Collins English Dictionary*, s.v. "seducer," accessed November 10, 2018, https://www.collinsdictionary.com/ us/dictionary/english/seducer.

7. genine, "Hola, Otras opciones: Casanova, Don Juan, Romeo, gigolo, heartbreaker, ladies' man, lady-killer, lecher, libertine, lothario, lover, lover-boy, rake, seducer, skirt chaser, stud*, wolf*," February 13, 2010, comment on Edmelisa, "Es Muy Perro," WordReference. com, https://forum.wordreference.com/threads/es-muy-perro.1699971/.

8. Thesaurus.com, s.v. "seductress," accessed November 10, 2018, https://www.thesaurus.com/browse/ seductress?s=t.

9. John Paul Jackson, *Unmasking the Jezebel Spirit* (Flower Mound, TX: Streams Creative House, 2014), 46.

10. Dictionary.com, s.v. "manipulation," accessed November 10, 2018, https://www.dictionary.com/browse/ manipulation?s=t.

11. Dictionary.com, s.v. "manipulate," accessed November 10, 2018, https://www.dictionary.com/browse/ manipulate?s=t.

Chapter 8: Destiny Road

1. WordReference.com, s.v. "restrain," accessed November 11, 2018, http://www.wordreference.com/definition/ restrain.

2. WordReference.com, s.v. "perish," accessed November 11, 2018, http://www.wordreference.com/definition/perish.

3. "English IV Vocab—Synonyms," Quizlet, accessed November 11, 2018, https://quizlet.com/6222365 /english-iv-vocab-synonyms-flash-cards/.

4. WordReference.com, s.v. "dwarf," accessed November 11, 2018, http://www.wordreference.com/definition/dwarfed.

5. *Random House Kernerman Webster's College Dictionary*, s.v. "procrastinate," accessed November 11, 2018, https://www.thefreedictionary.com/procrastinate.

Chapter 9: The Lie of Independence

1. Dictionary.com, s.v. "fornication," accessed November 11, 2018, https://www.dictionary.com/browse/fornication?s=t.

2. *Random House Kernerman Webster's College Dictionary*, s.v. "adultery," accessed November 11, 2018, https://www.the freedictionary.com/adultery.

3. Dictionary.com, s.v. "infidelity," accessed November 11, 2018, https://www.dictionary.com/browse/infidelity?s=t.

4. Dictionary.com, s.v. "fidelity," accessed November 11, 2018, https://www.dictionary.com/browse/fidelity?s=t. "Conjugal faithfulness" is fidelity.

5. Dictionary.com, s.v. "accountability," accessed November 11, 2018, https://www.dictionary.com/browse/accountability?s=t.

Chapter 10: Heritage Theft

1. "Fetal Development From Conception to Birth," National Right to Life, accessed November 11, 2018, https://nrlc.org/archive/abortion/facts/fetaldevelopment.html.

2. "Federal Laws That Protect Bald Eagles," US Fish and Wildlife Service, updated August 29, 2018, https://www.fws.gov/midwest/eagle/protect/laws.html.

3. "Questions and Answers About Bald Eagles Recovery and Delisting," U.S. Fish and Wildlife Service, revised October 2012, https://www.fws.gov/midwest/eagle/recovery/qandas.html.

4. "Bald Eagle (*Haliaeetus leucocephalus*)," Alaska Department of Fish and Game, accessed November 11, 2018,

http://www.adfg.alaska.gov/index.cfm?adfg=baldeagle.
main.

5. Blue Letter Bible, s.v. *"yada`,"* accessed November 11,
2018, https://www.blueletterbible.org//lang/lexicon
/lexicon.cfm?Strongs=H3045&t=KJV.

Chapter 11: The Jesus Addendum

1. Dictionary.com, s.v. "addendum," accessed November 11,
2018, https://www.dictionary.com/browse/addendum.

Chapter 13: A New Breed

1. Dictionary.com, s.v. "jealous," accessed November 11,
2018, https://www.dictionary.com/browse/jealous.
2. Dictionary.com, s.v. "offense," accessed November 11,
2018, https://www.dictionary.com/browse/offense?s=t.
3. Dictionary.com, s.v. "derail," accessed November 11,
2018, https://www.dictionary.com/browse/derail?s=t.

Conclusion: The Next Step

1. Chad M. Mansbridge, *He Qualifies You!* (n.p.: Seraph Creative, 2016), loc. 150–151, Kindle.

More From This Author

Mission Accomplished
The Secrets of Successful Missions

Mission Accomplished takes you
on a Bible-based journey
that will convince you
it's time to get out of the pew
and into the mission field.
Then, with humor, compassion and common sense,
Pratt gives you the tools with which to do it.

Now Available at
amazon.com

Platform Building Series
How To Expand Your Influence

It's all about the potential of YOUR BRAND
Why you need it, how to
walk through the process of building it,
and some powerful tools to aid
in creating and building your brand.
This is a "how-to" series
for making your brand a successful reality!

Follow Ron Pratt on social media
@PapaBearAlaska

And interact with him
on his LiveStream Broadcasts

For Business Inquiries:

Schedule Ron Pratt
for your next Men's Retreat,
Youth Conference,
Missions Work Shop or Missions Service.

Mailing Address:
P.O. Box 55761, North Pole, Alaska 99705
E-mail: RonPrattAlaska@gmail.com
Website: RonPrattAlaska.com
Learn more about **This Generation Ministries**
at **tgmALASKA.com**